i

Tell Them They Are Chosen

A strategy for mentoring, parenting, teaching,
coaching, leading, and ministry

By Ben Erickson

Cover design and photography – Brendin Nilsen

Daryl,

You have embraced me,
given me a vision for who I could
be in Christ, and inspired me with your
example and enthusiasm!

One of your "boys,"

Ben Culman

iii

Dedication

I am sincerely thankful for those who have prompted and supported me in writing this book.

God's mercy, grace and inspiration;

My wife, Marqua, my two lovely daughters, Kristi (and husband Carl) and Tessa, and five awesome granddaughters, Amanda, Peyton, Madison, Lauren, and Mickela;

My former students, athletes, and youth group kids, whose experiences have taught me more than I have taught them. Many of whom I have embraced; I have envisioned; I have inspired; To those whom I have failed to do so, I ask forgiveness.

The prayers of my Christian grandparents who believed God had His hand on my life.

My parents, Magnus and Marian who with God's direction helped shape me into who I am.

Note: The names of former students, athletes, and youth group kids have been changed in the stories I tell in this book. (If any of you read these stories you will know who you are. You obviously made an impression on me.)

Table of Contents

Imagine

*However, as it is written: "What no eye has
seen, what no ear has heard, and what no
human mind has conceived"— the things
God has prepared for those who love him—
1 Corinthians 2:9 (NIV)*

What would happen if every child of God knew
their life purpose and lived it out? I have thought
about that question a great deal. I know that the
world would be radically changed for the better.
God's Kingdom would be growing at an
incredible rate. People's lives would be joyfully
filled with significance. Each day would be lived
with great expectation and excitement for what
God was going to do through you and your
neighbors. We each would know what God had
created us to be and do.

Churches often call to the front and pray for
those people called to go into the mission field or
anoint someone for church work. What if each
week a different group of people, who are called
by God to a "secular" career, were anointed and
commissioned?

One week we could bless plumbers; the next, public school personnel; the next, medical professionals; the next, stay-at-home moms, the next, students. Imagine each Christian blessed and excited to glorify God through their job and neighborhood.

In the 2013 winter edition of *Leadership Journal,* Skye Jethani wrote an article, *Uncommon Callings,* in which he imagined such a world.

> *"Imagine a Christian community where followers of Christ are not merely focused upon church-based programs, but where they are taught how to commune with Christ and glorify and serve him where ever the individuals are called—in business, the trades, the arts, medicine, education, or elsewhere. Such a church would exist not to advance its own agenda, but to advance the common good. The callings would be diverse, occurring in different parts of the world, and in various channels of the culture, but every calling would be held in esteem by the church as coming from Christ and as part of his redemption of all things.*
>
> *As Christians are equipped for these callings, their good works would not simply benefit the church but everything and everyone in the community.*

Imagine Christian educators bringing order, beauty, and abundance to schools so students and their families thrive. Imagine Christian business leaders cultivating companies that value people, pay them fairly, and steward natural resources.

Imagine Christian artists creating works of beauty that lift the spirits of those who have endured war or disease. Imagine Christian civic leaders passing just laws to ensure acts of evil are restrained and life-giving order is possible."

I believe that this is possible! I believe that this can start happening now!

For that to happen we need to commit ourselves to nurturing the young people whom God has given to each of us.

We need to tell them they are chosen!
We need to embrace, envision and inspire the next generation to discover God's purpose for their lives.

Living with Purpose

"The Kingdom of God has come near."
Mark 1:15 (NIV)

"Your Kingdom come, your will be done, on earth as it is in heaven"
Matthew 6:10 (NIV)

Jesus declared God's Kingdom was here nearly two thousand years ago. He asked that we pray for its presence to grow and develop here on earth now, as well as to look forward to its future completion with a "new heaven and earth."

Too often we try to "sell" Christianity only as a "ticket to heaven" and an alternative to hell. We forget that, for Christians, we can experience the Kingdom of God now! We can experience significance, accomplishment and joy in this present world.

As a matter of fact, we are created with a specific purpose to grow his Kingdom with the life we are given. As we live this life purpose, we glorify the God who created us.

"For we are God's masterpiece, He has created us anew in Christ Jesus, so we can do the good things he planned for us long ago."
Ephesians 2:10 (NLT)

My Story

"For you have been my hope, Sovereign Lord, my confidence since my youth. From birth I have relied on you; you brought me forth from my mother's womb.I will ever praise you."
Psalm 71:5-6 (NIV)

I didn't hear the story until I was in my mid-thirties. My dad was sitting at the table in the kitchen and we were just having a cup of coffee.

I don't remember the context of the conversation we were having, but somehow the topic of my birth came up. Dad became a bit agitated and said that "now days we would sue that doctor." I didn't know what he meant. So I asked. That's when the story unfolded.

My mother had been previously married for eight years before my dad came along and was not able to have children. When she married my dad (In March of 1946), there was only a little hope that babies were possible.

In the fall of 1946, my mom started getting sick. My dad said she must be pregnant. The doctor ran whatever tests were available at that time and they all came back negative. The diagnosis was that there was a tumor. So in December of 1946, they performed surgery to remove it. Well to everyone's surprise, except my dad of course, they discovered me! They quickly sewed my mother back up. I was born the following June.

As I reflected on the seriousness of major surgery on a mother carrying a three-month old fetus, I realized that I was indeed a miracle baby!

I have been a Christian for as long as I can remember, but this story brought to culmination a sense that I had been born for a reason, a God-ordained purpose that was becoming clearer. I began to see patterns and trends in how God had gifted me with talents, experiences and passions. This story was the beginning of my life purpose journey.

> *"Since my youth, God, you have taught me, and to this day I declare your marvelous deeds. Even when I am old and gray,do not forsake me, my God,till I declare your power to the next generation,your mighty acts to all who are to come."*
> *Psalm 71:17-18 (NIV)*

God has blessed me with a full career of ministry. I taught and coached at the high school level; I was a junior high school counselor; and I have served in two different congregations as a youth pastor. In the late 1990's I read a book by Laurie Beth Jones titled *The Path*. In this book, I was guided to come up with my personal mission statement. As I looked at who I was and what God had me doing for over twenty years, I came up with this: **to Embrace, Envision and Inspire the love of God in today's youth.** God has used me to love kids, show them a vision for life and inspire them through encouragement, example and celebration.

As I neared my retirement as a youth pastor in 2012, God led me to realize that **my ministry (mission) was now to become my message**. This book is the actualization of that call.

Please join me as we discover what God had in mind for us, particularly in reaching the next generation.

The Strategy

This book is a strategy to tell the next generation that they are chosen by God. This is a **strategy for mentoring, parenting, teaching, coaching, leading, and ministry.**

7

I have been asked, "Could a young person read this, or is it just for the adults working with them?" I will answer by telling a story. When I was in graduate school for my Masters in counseling, one of the books assigned was *How to Talk So Kids will Listen and Listen So Kids Will Talk* by Adele Faber, Elaine Mazlick and Kimberly Ann Coe. I spotted my sixteen-year-old daughter reading it several times. On a Friday night, she was going to take our car out with her friends. She asked. "Dad, what time do you want me home?" Using a technique set forth in the book, I said, "What time do <u>you</u> think you should be home?" She rolled her eyes and said, "Dad, quit trying to be a good parent and just tell me what time to come home." She very well understood what the book said and came to her own very mature conclusion.

We tell the next generation that they are chosen by . . .
- **Embracing** them!
- Helping them **envision** their life purpose.
- **Inspiring** them on that journey!

The next generation needs to be loved and **embraced**. By embraced, I mean the whole breadth of Gods' unconditional love.

We need to see each emerging adult as someone who is loved by God and envelope them with all the kindness and care that we can muster. This applies to every kid, the embraceable as well as the seemingly un-embraceable.

Young people need a **vision**. They need to be shown who this Jesus guy is. The reality is we have a loving and forgiving God, who died for us. He showed us a way to live that is impossibly challenging, yet possible through a relationship with Him. In that relationship, they will need to see that with suffering comes growth, with sacrifice comes joy, and with mercy comes grace. **They need to see that God has created them for a specific purpose and that they are uniquely qualified to accomplish that purpose**. In that purpose, as difficult as that may be, they will find peace, joy and God's blessing.

Each young adult needs **inspiration**. They need to be encouraged in their journey. They need a solid, Christ-like example of humility, wisdom, and sacrifice. They need a role model; someone who is a true follower of Jesus, who passionately worships his God and compassionately loves his neighbor.

This strategy is how I have ministered to youth for over 44 years. It has given me a focus and a purpose for my life.

My message to you is that this strategy can be used by anyone who is in a leadership position and wishes to positively influence the next generation.

A Place to start . . . a new mindset.

As a school counselor, I would go into classrooms and do a three to five day career unit. The primary goal was to get the kids thinking about a future career.

I wanted to help them relate their future goals to their upcoming signups for next year's schedule of classes. I would always start by asking, **"What do you want to be when you grow up?"** The kids would begin to squirm and a few would raise their hands and have an answer. (In 8th grade, the careers most mentioned were professional athlete, musician, or movie star.)

I would then ask, **"How many of you hate that question?"** All the hands would go up! Why? Because when the kids were younger the answer was easy and very imaginative. But by eighth grade, it has become more serious and there is pressure and expectations from school, parents and the community to make a commitment to actually do something about a career choice.

Then I would follow up by telling them that it really is the **wrong question**. I would tell them that before you can answer the question about what you want to be, you have to ask the question, "**Who are you?**" and/or "**Who are you becoming?**

This became the lead-in to an inventory that would give the kids insight into their personalities, skills, abilities and passions. The follow-up discussions then became an exciting exploration of themselves and how that might lead to a career that would fit who they are.

Discovering our journey in life is really discovering who God has made us to be (His masterpiece). Our gifts, passions, skills and even our experiences, all can show us where God might be leading.

We, as adults, also ask the wrong questions.

When meeting someone for the first time the dialogue usually goes like this . . .
"Hi, my name is John."
"Hi, I'm Ben."
"What do you do, Ben?"
When I hear that question, I am tempted to answer, " Well, I listen to my wife a lot. I do whatever my grandkids want, and I do as little real work as I can get away with." (Now that I am retired, I may actually start to use those lines.)

I know that the question is about what job or career I have and I usually answer accordingly. I do this because I am a polite, non-offending kind of guy.

What I would like to say is . . . "I hate that question! Why is that the job question comes up right after you know my name? Does the job or career that I have really define me? Am I not more than my job?

How refreshing and astonishing it would be for them to say . . .
"Who are you? Ben, I would really like to know the real you."

After a moment of shock, I would joyfully respond by saying . . . I am a happily married husband, a part time father (they are adults now), a proud and active grandfather, a great listener and friend, a full time disciple of Jesus (and I disciple others). I also enjoy reading, biking, hiking, photography and riding my motorcycle. I think sharing barbeque and good conversation with my family and friends is a great way to end a day. And by the way, I have this very cool job that really fits me perfectly.

God has created each of us uniquely to accomplish a unique purpose. If we really embrace people and ask the right questions, we might discover what that unique purpose is.

Tell them they are God's Song.

Kids today are up on all the lyrics to their favorite songs. They sing along with ease because they have memorized the words. This is true for traditional song lyrics as well as many of the rap lyrics. Many teens even love to write their own rap lyrics. These kids enjoy the message that is expressed in these lyrics. They even adopt these songs as "their own". The message becomes their message.

Did you know that God is sending a message to the world through you? You are God's song lyrics. The word "masterpiece" in the following verse (workmanship in some translations) can be correctly translated as "poem" or song lyric.

> *"For we are God's masterpiece, He has created us anew in Christ Jesus, so we can do the good things he planned for us long ago." Ephesians 2:10 (NLT)*

Just as each song is distinctive and carries a different message than other songs, so you have a unique message that God is trying to communicate through you.

You are God's song, created in Christ Jesus, so that you can sing and dance the way He planned long ago.

How then, as a parent or coach or mentor, are we to guide a young person? In the following chapters, we will see that by **embracing** our youth, **envisioning** who God is and who they are and **inspiring** them, they will discover what God's purpose for their life. We will tell they are chosen!

A Note on Obstacles

In any "How to" book, one must consider obstacles. Even if you learn "how to" do something, you may have reasons for not doing what you know needs to be done. Reasons like . . .

> I am not qualified to do this.
> Someone else could do this better.
> I need more training before I can actually do this.

Again the whole purpose of this book is to let you know that God is really in charge of each of these questions. He has created you, given you specific gifts and talents and experiences to qualify you. Others have their talents and tasks to perform. You may need to see how you can work in concert with those people. If you understand this as a process that takes patience, wisdom and discernment on your part and trust God's timing, God will give you the task when He thinks you are ready.

Lack of confidence, esteem, or worth and self-doubt are not from God. He will give you the strength, the wisdom, and love to influence the next generation.

I would tell you that YOU ARE CHOSEN to EMBRACE, ENVISION AND INSPIRE THE NEXT GENERATION!

To Embrace

"This is my command: Love each other."
John 15:17 (NIV)

Tell them they are chosen by embracing them!

I have always embraced kids, specifically junior and senior high kids. As a high school classroom teacher, I enjoyed being with them, hearing their stories and sharing with them my passion for learning. What kept me coming back to the classroom year after year was the relationships I had with my students.

Sometimes there were students who were discipline problems and I took pride in the fact that if I really worked on a positive relationship with them the discipline issues would decrease.

One day, the mother of one of these students called me at school and stated quite emphatically that her son was not doing well in my class because I didn't like him. I quickly assured her that it was his behavior that I didn't like and that in fact I did like him.

16

As I hung up, I realized that what she had said really hit me hard. It wasn't enough to know that I cared for her son. *He* had to know that I cared for him.

I was able to set aside some time to affirm to him that he was a funny, bright and charming young man. I liked him, but to the fairness of the other students and to me, he needed to bring those outgoing characteristics under control within the bounds of my classroom. This conversation didn't miraculously turn things around, but it helped. I had to work to show him that I really did care for him. This meant numerous "side conversations" where I tried to build on a positive relationship. I showed concern for his welfare both in and out of my classroom. I showed appreciation for his humor, his intelligence, and his talents.

This story and twenty years in a public school classroom have made me a firm believer in the adage; "They don't care what you know until they know you care."

So where does this love for kids come from?

It is obvious to me that some people simply don't like kids. Fortunately, I have not met many of those people in the field of education or youth work.

As a lifetime follower of Christ, I have spent some time seriously studying the Bible. While planning a lesson on the Fruits of the Spirit,

> *"But the fruit of the Spirit is love, joy, peace, forbearance, kindness, goodness, faithfulness, gentleness and self-control."*
> *Galatians 5:22-23 (NIV)*

I came across an interesting interpretation of the word "goodness." It indicated that "goodness" was more about seeing God (good) in other people than it was the quality of good in me. WOW! If I saw God in people, if I saw them as His creation, His image, would I not love them, accept them, forgive them, and care for them as God did? This character trait of goodness, this attitude about people, this ability to see other people in the light of God's mercy and grace grows out of His Spirit living in us, a fruit given to us to minister to others.

What effect would embracing "God in people" have on them? We love God because he first loved us.

> *"Dear friends, let us love one another, for love comes from God. Everyone who loves has been born of God and knows God. Whoever does not love does not know God, because God is love. This is how God showed his love among us: He sent his one and only Son into the world that we might*

*live through him. This is love: not that we
loved God, but that he loved us and sent his
Son as an atoning sacrifice for our sins.
Dear friends, since God so loved us, we also
ought to love one another. No one has ever
seen God; but if we love one another, God
lives in us and his love is made complete in
us."*
1 John 4:7-12 (NIV)

As such, we become the first "Gospel" that many
people read (before they read the Gospels of
Matthew, Mark, Luke or John). If they see love in
us, if they know we care, they become more and
more open to the Jesus who has given us that
love.

Hurting Kids

Chap Clark, in his book *Hurt* has documented the
abandonment of our youth by schools, parents,
churches and society in general. Having spent all
these years as a teacher, coach, school counselor
and youth pastor, I would confirm Clark's
assessment. Kids spend more time today without
adult care and less time hearing the good news
about who they are and who they could be than
when I was a teen. They spend more time in
front of a screen than being nurtured by a caring,
Christian adult.

Not long ago, I was teaching an "embrace" lesson
based on Ephesians 2:10.

For we are God's masterpiece. He has created us anew in Christ Jesus, so we can do the good things he planned for us long ago." (NLT)

At the end of my lesson introduction, I asked all the kids to stand and say out loud in unison, "I am God's masterpiece, chosen to change the world!" I got a halfhearted response. Was this a mistake?

I asked my small group leaders to have kids do the same thing in that more intimate setting. In our post-group leaders' meeting, I asked how that went over with the kids. One of my female leaders reported that with the girls, it was really not well received. One eighth grade girl reported, "This is really hard for me. We come to church and youth group and we hear that we are 'God's masterpiece.' We don't hear that message anyplace else."

It dawned on me that our youth's very identity is at stake here. I agree that many of our students have an attitude of entitlement. They feel they are "owed" something from our society. I believe, however, that this is more the result of the abandonment of these kids and a reflection of their poor self-esteem than it is that they think too highly of themselves.

We really do owe them something. They are "entitled" to know that they are created in God's image; that they are loved by God ("while they are yet sinners"); that God has a plan for their lives and that in God's eyes as well as our eyes they are "God's masterpiece, created and chosen to change the world for Christ."

Kids need to be embraced with the love of Christ. They need to know that they are chosen. That is our task, our strategy and our command from God.

Identity is Crucial - Who am I?

The standard "uniform" when I was in high school was a T shirt, blue jeans, tennis shoes (Converse All Stars) and for me and my crowd, a letterman's jacket. I don't remember it being a conscious decision to look like everyone else, but with that letterman's jacket I knew that it provided the status and identity that I thought was who I really was.

Being an athlete is still an important part of my identity, although I occasionally catch myself saying "former" athlete. When I do that I quickly "correct" it by saying that I still lift weights, ride a bike, swim and hike. (Am I a senior citizen in denial, or is it truly who I am?)

Finding our true identity is a process.

As we grow we discover things about ourselves that make us feel more comfortable, more alive, or more passionate. Discovering these traits may take a few years or a few decades of trial and error.

Because of the "error" part of the process, it is sometimes painful. This is like learning to walk. We fall down a lot. We skin a knee. We bang our head. It hurts. But eventually, we not only walk but we feel the joy of running.

Sometimes people resign themselves to being "nobody" important. God's word, however, is quite clear that we are "uniquely" important.

To again clarify the meaning of Ephesians 2:10, God's "masterpiece" can be translated "poiema/poem" or "song." **Our life purpose is to do the good things he planned for us long ago.**

We can each discover this purpose in an environment of love, by examining in detail our own uniqueness and with the encouragement and example of godly role models.

It is strange to think of ourselves as a "masterpiece" or "God's song." But that is the reality of it. If the God who created the universe, who gave His son to die for us, who raised him from the dead for us, says this, then who are we to argue? It is only for us to discover and reflect upon our personal "song" and to go about living it out.

Our life purpose must be discovered in the context of our relationship with Christ.

> *It's in Christ that we find out who we are and what we are living for. Long before we first heard of Christ and got our hopes up, he had his eye on us, had designs on us for glorious living, part of the overall purpose he is working out in everything and everyone.*
>
> *It's in Christ that you, once you heard the truth and believed it (this Message of your salvation), found yourselves home free— signed, sealed, and delivered by the Holy Spirit. This signet from God is the first installment on what's coming, a reminder that we'll get everything God has planned for us, a praising and glorious life.*
> *Ephesians 1:11-14 (MSG)*

It is in our relationship with God that we discover who we are meant to be. As we learn more about who He is, we discover who we are. He is our ultimate mentor and guide. He molds our character and leads us to live the life he intends for us.

Questions to Ponder

What was / is your "uniform"?

How did it / does it reflect your identity?

Have you ever tried to change your "image"? Clothes, hair, behavior?

What do you think it means <u>for you</u> to be God's Masterpiece (song)?

What makes you unique (besides fingerprints and DNA)?

What does God's love have to do with who I am?

What is it to embrace someone? (Way Beyond a Hug!)

Growing up, hugs were something I was not accustomed to or comfortable with. Not that I didn't get some, but neither of my parents nor their families were "huggers."

This all changed rather quickly when I married. My mother-in-law's family were all "huggers!" I had never been hugged so much as at our wedding reception. At first, this made me feel very uncomfortable.

And as the years passed, every time I would see one of my wife's aunts I was always greeted with a big hug. After a few years, I came to enjoy the warmth, affection and joy that came with these hugs. I became a "hugger!"

A hug is a glad expression of welcome, a caring expression of empathy and a warm expression of farewell. It says I love you!

When two people hug, they are making themselves vulnerable. By opening your arms, you are saying, "I trust you."

I need to interrupt for a moment. In our sexually charged environment, it is important to be really careful about hugging. One needs to be sensitive to the reaction of people to physical touch. As I would walk around the classroom, I would sometimes touch a student on the shoulder.

Interestingly, some would tense up and others would relax. Touch can mean different things to different people. Past experiences can make you react in different ways. It took me a while to learn to hug people whom I did not know very well. For an abuse victim, it is even more difficult.

I heard a story recently from a woman who had been kidnapped into the sex trade. When asked what prompted her to finally get out of this predicament, she said that a man looked her in the eye and smiled warmly. This look told her that she was a worthwhile person, not something to be bought and sold. She followed up and discovered this man was a pastor of a local church. Because someone embraced her with a warm look and a smile, she sought the help she needed.

You can even embrace people by shaking hands. As a counselor, this was one of my favorite ways to greet seventh grade boys into my office.

I would teach them how to do it warmly and firmly. (Not firmly enough to hurt a lady's hand and not a weak cold fish.) It was fun to see these boys eyes light up when I treated them like a young man.

Some people call a hug an embrace. And it definitely is. But to embrace someone is so much more than just a hug! It is to accept the other person as one of God's fellow creations. It is to see them as God sees them. It is to forgive them as God does. It is to delight in their uniqueness and celebrate their gifts, talents, and quirks. Sometimes it is to love them when they are quite unlovable.

When you embrace someone, you seek to bring out the best in him or her. You see their potential and encourage them to grow. You nurture them.

If you truly are embracing another, they can feel the warmth and positive regard that you have for them.

It was only after I embraced the youth I worked with that I was able to influence their lives. Actually, when you have truly embraced them, they hug you!

Many times the "embracing" was the most important influence of all. When you know you are loved, it changes who you are.

The Joy of Relationships

Embracing is about building relationships. When you are embraced, it opens up joy in those relationships.

Richard was one of our top athletes. He was student body president. He was a in my Urban Studies class and shared some painful experiences he had as a black student in a mostly white community.

I was standing in the hall between classes when he passed by. I said, "Hi, Richard." He replied, "Hi, Mr. Sawyer (my colleague)." I corrected him with, "Mr. Erickson." He smiled and said, "All you social studies teachers look alike." We both burst in to laughter. I knew that I had successfully "embraced" him.

Miriam was a Jewish student in my American History class. When I was teaching about religion in our country, she said she could bring some information from home to share with the class. She ended up teaching my classes for a couple of days. I embraced her and her teaching. She later brought some Hanukah cookies from home and offered me one. I told her they tasted just like Christmas cookies to me! That spring, my wife and I were invited to her house for Passover. As I embraced her, her family embraced mine.

Trust in Relationship

By embracing people, we can earn their trust. Trust is taught by being trustworthy.

One year, I had a unique situation on our football team. I had two offensive guards who were both very good.

I had two backup guards who were so close in ability that it was impossible to say which was better. As a matter of fact, all four were very close. One of the starters got hurt and was going to be out for several weeks.

I called the two back ups and the one remaining starter into my office. I said that I could not decide who would fill the open spot. I told them I wanted to rotate all three of them every play so that all three would have equal playing time. I also told them that they would be in charge of which two would start and how the rotation would happen. I told them that I had other things I needed to worry about during the game and I wanted them to do this automatically without checking with me.

They were a bit shocked that I wasn't going to name a starter. (You should know that starting is a "big deal" to players.) They weren't sure that they trusted me to keep this deal going in the following games. They, somewhat reluctantly, said that they would give this a try.

Over the next few games they decided the starters and the rotation of the three of them. It worked really well. As they learned to trust that I would not interfere with what they were doing, they developed and amazing chemistry between them and pride in what they were accomplishing.

After three or four weeks the injured player was ready to come back. I called them all into my office and asked how they were going to deal with that issue. They quickly answered that it would now be a four-man rotation instead of three. The importance of starting and playing time – instead of being in on two-thirds of the plays, they each would only get one-half of the plays – became less important than being part of a very special group on the team. Because I embraced them, they trusted me; and had an amazing bonding experience with their fellow offensive guards.

Trust comes when you embrace people. Will was our long snapper for punts and extra points. He took pride in making a great snap each time. We all embraced Will as a critical part of our team.

One game, we had a six point lead late in the game. We were in a fourth down situation on our own five-yard line. We called a time out. My offensive coordinator and I decided we would take an intentional safety, giving them two points and hopefully putting them into a situation with too far to go with too little time.

We called Will over to the sidelines and told him to snap the ball high over the punters head and out the back of the end zone.

He just stared at us. I said, "Will, do you understand what we want you to do?" He replied, "OK coach, but you're going to have to explain this to my mom!" He trusted us because he knew we had cared for him.

Sometimes it's the little things that count. My wife was returning home from the grocery store. As she neared a friend's house, she felt called to stop by and see her. They chatted for about an hour and my wife came home. The next day at church, the lady, who was recently divorced, pulled my wife aside and thanked her for stopping by and saving her life! She said, "I was going to commit suicide, but when you came by, I realized life was worth living."

What enables me to embrace others?

Sometimes I don't like myself very much. Sometimes I hate the things I think and do. I still know that God loves me, but do I love myself? In John 3, we are told that "God so loved the world . . ." and I realize that means me also. In Luke 10, Jesus calls us to . . . "Love your neighbor as yourself."

How can I really love myself?
First I need to see how God sees me?
   I am His "masterpiece". Ephesians 2:10
   For I am made in God's image. Genesis 1:27
   God knew me even before I was conceived.
   Jeremiah 1:4-5

He chose me when He planned creation. Ephesians 1:11-12

I am not a mistake, for all my days are written in God's book. Psalm 139:15-16

I am fearfully and wonderfully made. Psalm 139:14

God's plan for my future has always been filled with hope. Jeremiah 29:11

God loves me with an everlasting love. Jeremiah 31:3

God's thoughts toward me are countless as the sand on the seashore.Psalms 139:17-18

And God rejoices over me with singing. Zephaniah 3:17

I am God's treasured possession. Exodus 19:5

He desires to establish mewith all His heart and soul. Jeremiah 32:41

God is my greatest encourager. 2 Thessalonians 2:16-17

He is also the Father who comforts me in all my troubles. 2 Corinthians 1:3-4

When I am brokenhearted, He is close to me. Psalm 34:18

He is my Father, and He loves me even as He loves His son, Jesus. John 17:23

For in Jesus, God's love for me is revealed. John 17:26

And to tell me that He is not counting my sins.2 Corinthians 5:18-19

Jesus died so that God and I could be reconciled. 2 Corinthians 5:18-19

His death was the ultimate expression of His love for me. 1 John 4:10
He gave up everything He lovedthat He might gain my love. Romans 8:31-32
And nothing will ever separate me from God's love again. Romans 8:38-39

I stated earlier that, "when you know you are loved, it changes who you are."

Knowing that I am loved gives me assurance. It gives me confidence that I have a purpose. As I grow in that "love" knowledge, it gives me worth. It gives me the encouragement I need to reach out and share that love with my "neighbor."

God doesn't physically "hug" us, but through His Word and His Holy Spirit, he really does embrace us with his love. I believe that I am changed by God's love to see myself as He sees me and in turn love others.

"We love each other because he loved us first." 1 John 4:19 (NIV)

The Strategy of Embracing

If we tell them they are chosen then we need to choose them!

As a kid I loved baseball. I still do. Although I played a year or two of little league, most of my baseball memories are from "sandlot" ball.

It wasn't exactly sand. We built a backstop in our cow pasture and used blocks of wood for bases. I learned to hook slide to avoid cow pies.

In cow pasture ball, you choose up sides! Being chosen first was always a great ego boost. Being chosen last, not so much. It was recognition that you were not skilled enough, big enough or strong enough. Somehow we survived with our egos intact.

Previously I referred to Chap Clark's book *Hurt 2.0,* about how kids today are abandoned. I think that "abandoned" is at least one step below being "not chosen."

To be chosen is a special recognition that we are somehow worthy; that there is a purpose for our being: that we are capable of contributing to others.

The really good news (Gospel) is that we are "chosen by God."

> *"You did not choose me, but I **chose you** and **appointed** you to go and bear fruit— fruit that will last. Then the Father will give you whatever you ask in my name."*
> *John 15:16 (NIV)*

> *"For we know, brothers loved by God, that he has **chosen** you,"*
> *1 Thessalonians 1:4 (NIV)*

*"For he **chose** us in him before the creation of the world to be holy and blameless in his sight."* Ephesians 1:4 (NIV)

In a world where people are hurt, lost, and abandoned, being chosen by the Creator of the universe for a specific reason can lead to a realization of self worth and life purpose.

Questions to Ponder

Have you ever been chosen last or even left out altogether?
How did that feel?
How does it feel to know that God chooses you for a specific purpose?
Have you discovered what you have been chosen for?
Have you told anyone that they are chosen by God?
How do you think they might react?

We need to see them as God sees them!

I have spent most of my career as a teacher in the public schools. With the advent of the Americans with Disabilities Act, teachers have been asked to teach a widening range of abilities and talents. The fact that some of these kids have very low levels of intellectual capacity and that the creation of Special Education classrooms is costly, has left some teachers frustrated. To what purpose, to what benefit do we provide a costly education for these kids?

I was recently given an opportunity to be a substitute teacher in a classroom with Autistic and Downs Syndrome kids. As I spent time with the teachers and kids, I pondered, What life purpose do these kids serve? When I finished the three weeks in this class, I wrote the following email to the head teacher.

"I just spent three weeks in a special needs classroom at a your junior high.

Concerning the education of these kids, I have heard people ask, "What productive purpose do these kids have? Will they ever contribute to our world? Are they not a burden on parents, teachers, school systems and society in general?"

As I spent time with these kids and their adult educators, I thought about these kids and their "purpose" in life. In the classroom, wonderful caring adults work with these kids on a daily basis. They teach reading, math, writing, social skills, hygiene and work skills to these "special" young people. In reality though, they learn way more than they teach!

What if God's purpose for my life was . . .
To influence people to love more;
To show people that simple things matter;
To help people appreciate their blessings;

To help people understand the blessings of giving of themselves;
To show childlike smiles, laughter and tears without any social masks;
To challenge people to look past the obvious to the discernable;
To help people see each other as God sees them;
To let my dependence give purpose to other's independence;
For my life purpose to supply your life purpose!

Would not that be a life well lived? Would it matter that I wouldn't realize that I had this influence on others?

I believe that all people have special needs and special gifts with which God has blessed us. My special need may indeed be a special gift to others. My special gift may be to meet your special need. We both embrace and are embraced by these kids. They show us a vision for a truly purposeful life. They inspire our growth and encourage our lives."

I had written the email to the teachers and para-educators in that classroom to support and encourage their work with these kids.

I immediately received her reply. She said that my email had come at the right time. Some faculty had expressed their frustration to the school principal. I then forwarded my email to the principal and the whole staff.

My purpose was to help the staff to see these kids as God sees them and understand that these special kids have an important life purpose. I was humbled by the response from staff members. The email had provided a positive new view on some of the school's most precious students.

Questions to Ponder

Are there any "special needs" people in your life? How do they affect the life purpose of those around them?
What special gifts do they offer to you?
What special needs or special gifts do you have?

We need to embrace the un-embraceable: Extra Grace Required (EGR)

Some kids (people) are just hard to love! One such kid was Tommy. His behavior was very self-centered. In the classroom, he was busy chatting and laughing to the point of disrupting other students and would react with anger or disrespect when he was asked to change his behavior. His immediate comeback was that the teacher didn't "like" him and was picking on him. He saw no "purpose" in doing what he was told.

So how do you deal with people like Tommy? One answer I have heard from teachers is that your have to start out as a "tough disciplinarian" with kids and then "ease up" later. This "Don't smile until November" strategy may in fact sabotage what you are trying to accomplish. In my experience you will lose many kids; they will give up on you and themselves in the process. You have sent the message that "I don't like you!" (The student reacts with "I don't like you either! Therefore I will ignore your message.") A belief that the teacher doesn't like me is very hard to change. The kids put up a wall. They openly share with teachers they like the names of teachers who are "mean" to them. A teacher friend, who embraces her kids from day one, told me she uses that to help discipline her students when needed. She simply states, "You don't want me to talk to you like those other teachers talk to you do you? They quickly behave. They want to be treated with care and respect.

If you can embrace students by seeking to understand who they are (seeing them as God sees them) and loving them despite their behavior, you will have a chance to see real change. They need to know first that you are glad they are there and secondly that you have behavior expectations for them.

They need to hear . . .

"I really like you, but your behavior disappoints me. I know you can do better." (Your disappointment tells them they are worthy of better. Your anger tells them they are not.)
"I see a purpose for your life."
"I see you as a unique individual."
"I like you because of who you are and who you can become."

Envision a positive future for them and never forget that your enthusiasm and encouragement is inspirational.

They will test you on this. They will need more reminders. They will need progressive discipline. (You will have to repeatedly explain this.) To be successful, these kids will require extra grace on your part. It will require an immense amount of patience. It may be exhausting! But if you persist, it can also be extremely fulfilling for you and life-changing for the young person.
If God's extra grace has changed your life, you need to ask Him to help it to overflow to others.

If you can be consistent and persistent with this grace, if you can be consistent and persistent with your expectations, you may, with God's help, be the one person to make a real difference in their life.

I was recently made aware of a strategy that illustrates what I am talking about. Angela Watson on her blog *The Cornerstone* relayed an idea from the *Encouraging Teachers Facebook Group*. It is called *The 2 x 10 Strategy*. It simply says to talk to an at-risk kid for two minutes a day for ten days straight about anything she or he wants to talk about. The are getting astounding results. Remember; "They don't care what you know until they know that you care!"

Questions to ponder

Are there people like Tommy (EGRs) in your life?
Can you have high expectations for people and embrace them at the same time?
Is God's grace in your life apparent to you?
Is God's grace in you obvious to others?

We need to be present in their lives.

We cannot embrace our young people if we are absent. Their purpose is discovered in the embracing presence of God as experienced through our embracing presence.

In my work with young people, my message was always: You are loved! You are chosen! You are God's masterpiece!

What is the message from parents, teachers, coaches and other adults to our young people? Chap Clark, in his book, *Hurt 2.0*, calls **abandonment "the defining issue for contemporary adolescence."** Our kids see us as "absent!"

A few thousand years ago, the people of Israel felt abandoned. They lived in exile as slaves. God spoke to them through the person of Jeremiah.

> *"I know the plans I have for you, plans to prosper you and not to harm you, plans to give you hope and a future. You will call upon me and come and pray to me and I will listen to you. You will seek me and find me and when you seek me with all your heart. I will be found by you!"*
> *Jeremiah 29:11-14 (NIV)*

This is an excerpt from a letter written by Jeremiah to these "abandoned" people. In this letter, he promises God's presence. In this letter, he embraces who they are in God's eyes. In this letter, he tells them they are important in the plans that God has for the world.

Questions to Ponder

Could you write (with God's help) a letter (email, text, tweet) to a young person who feels the abandonment so prevalent in our culture?

Can you be "present" in the life of someone who needs to hear they are God's masterpiece? What might that look like?

Showing up!

Again, We cannot embrace our young people if we are absent.

As a football coach, we used to have a "Dad's Night" where the father of the player would wear the "away" jersey and join the team on the sideline for a home game. Shortly after announcing this to our team, there was a knock on the coach's office door. "Coach, can my mom wear my jersey on Friday?" Quickly realizing this player's father was long gone in this kid's life, we agreed. His mom could wear the jersey. A minute later another knock came and then a third. "Could my brother wear my jersey?" "Could my sister wear my jersey?"

Seeing where this was going, we immediately called a team meeting. We announced that any person that the player wanted to represent them was welcome to join us on the sideline wearing the jersey. "Dad's Night" became "Family Night." "Family" was defined as broadly as possible. It included all who support, embrace, stand up for and love you.

We often have the opportunity to show up in young people's lives. Showing up for concerts, games, back to school nights or even just hanging out with a kid can make a huge difference in their life. If we show up in a kid's life, they may even ask if we would wear their jersey. What an honor!

Questions to Ponder

How could you "show up" in the life of someone this week?
Who would be excited to see you there?

We need to listen to them!

The highest compliment you can pay anyone is to listen. It is the best strategy ever to establish and maintain a relationship. It says; "You are important! I care about what you have to say and therefore, I care about you!"

Listening does not problem solve. It does not need you to respond with your thoughts, opinions or advice. It sits in focused attention on the speaker and loves them.

Active listening does clarify meaning. It does reflect thoughts and feelings. It may even ask questions. But it does so without judgment. It has no agenda but to understand and love the person who is sharing.

My favorite story about this listening relationship is from a 1980's interview of Mother Theresa by news anchor Dan Rather.

> **Rather** – *"What do you say to God when you pray?"*
>
> **Mother Theresa** – *"I don't say anything. I listen."*
>
> **Rather** – *"Then what does Jesus say to you?"*
>
> **Mother Theresa** – *"He doesn't say anything either. He just listens!"*
>
> **She then added** *"If you don't understand that, I can't explain it to you."*

To really embrace someone you must listen to not only their words, but to their body language and their emotions. If you can reflect those things back to them, they will feel embraced. It will open the door to an even deeper conversation.

Young people are hungry for someone to really listen to their hearts. It will amaze you how they can process and even solve their own issues when they feel they are deeply heard. Listening is the fertile soil in which people grow and discover who they are and what their life purpose is.

We need to speak into their lives and affirm them.

Words are powerful! God created the universe by speaking! *"And God said . . ."* is repeated seven times in the first chapter of the Bible. Jesus is the "Word" that became flesh.

Likewise, the words we use with others can and do have a powerful influence. "Sticks and stones can break my bones, but words will never hurt me." We often repeat this lie when we are children, usually in response to teasing. As we grow up, we soon learn that words really do hurt. As a junior high counselor, I have handed Kleenex to too many kids whose hearts were broken by words said to them; only a few tears were from a physical injury.

Small children under five take words literally. Words used to describe them are the literal truth. In their young eyes, their parents cannot lie to them. Both positive and negative names are literal truth to a child. Teachers, peers, coaches and others then reinforce these words in their lives. These words are carried forward to adulthood and become part of who they are. Our self-image is created by these words. It is not hard to understand why a young teen would find it uncomfortable or incomprehensible to be described as a "masterpiece."

On the other hand, words can also create a confident and competent adult who "loves others as one loves oneself."

As I previously noted, my dad and my mom always described me as smart, capable and responsible, that I could accomplish whatever I set my mind to.

As I took on those qualities, others would comment and reinforce as well as build on these words. I remember in ninth grade as I was leaving the locker room on the last day of school, my football coach called out, "Hey Erickson, see you on the varsity next fall." I thought, "Well if he thinks I can then maybe I can."

I entered the fall with confidence and I did make the varsity. I gained some experience that year, started as a junior and senior in high school and lettered for four years at Pacific Lutheran University. I coached football for 27 years! Words are indeed powerful. They help create who we are and influence who we become.

We need to invite them!

Part of embracing people is to invite them. Inviting someone is to become vulnerable. It is welcoming them to your turf. It is being present with them.

It is sharing resources, time, maybe even money. It is offering something of yourself: your skills, your knowledge, your passion, your creativity, your love. It means asking if you can be invited into their lives; being present at their games, performances, and other events.

Questions to Ponder

Is there an area where you can serve them; help with academics, mentoring, or just listening over a cup of coffee?

Can you invite them to get involved in what you're doing? A teacher might invite a student to help a younger child. A coach might invite an athlete for one on one coaching after practice. A leader might invite a follower to attend a special workshop. A parent might invite their child to help make dinner. A counselor might invite a client to reach out to someone else. A mentor might invite a mentee to coffee.

The only agenda for these invitations is to embrace the person, to make them feel special by your presence, because they are special!

Conclusion

We need to tell them they are chosen. To embrace the next generation is hard work, but it is the work that we are commanded to do.

We need to choose them. We need to see them as God sees them. We need to embrace the un-embraceable as well as the embraceable. We need to be persistent in our love. We need to be present in their lives. We need to listen to them. We need to speak into their lives. We need to affirm them. We need to invite them.

To Envision

"Where there is no vision, the people perish." Proverbs 29:18a (KJV)

"I ask—ask the God of our Master, Jesus Christ, the God of glory—to make you intelligent and discerning in knowing him personally, your eyes focused and clear, so that you can see exactly what it is he is calling you to do." Ephesians 1:17-18 (MSG)

Tell them they are chosen by helping them envision their life purpose!

What is our purpose in this life we lead? What are we called to do? Can I really find meaning and joy beyond just trying to simply survive?

We have several calls in our lives. Our greatest calls are to . . .
1. To love God with all you have
2. To love your neighbor as yourself

These are universal. They are the same for each of us.

There is a third call and it is different. It is for us alone! We have a life purpose that God has created us specifically to accomplish.

> "For we are God's masterpiece, He has created us anew in Christ Jesus, so we can do the good things he planned for us long ago." Ephesians 2:10 (NLT)

Your life purpose; can you see it? Can you bring it into focus? Seeing this future vision doesn't always happen overnight. It could take twenty years or more. Abraham and Moses were eighty years old when they heard the call from God. God is at work here and He is changing you, readying you, for the job that He has for you. It requires listening to God. It entails responding to God's prompts. It means taking steps of faith and listening some more.

We need to discover who we are, how we are each a masterpiece of God's creative genius. He has things for us to do and he has given us the tools to do them.

What are my aptitudes, my strengths, my gifts, my passions? How has my life to this point prepared me for this? Are there future experiences that will further prepare me? Has God given me a dream for this future? Has He given me a burden for a certain situation, a certain people, a certain place? Have I found joy when I have responded to those burdens?

N. T. Wright says that we need to . . .

> *"Listen to the prophetic call of God, and to the pain of the present world, and to live at the point of intersection between the two." Mark for Everyone (a commentary) on Mark 6:7-13*

To Envision means to picture something mentally; to see it in your mind's eye.

To Envision . . .

> Seeing how you are uniquely created.
> Knowing God's specific purpose for your life.
> Meeting the "pain of this present world" with all the gifts that God has given you.
> Seeing and feeling the blessings and joy in you and others.

Now envision this for each follower of Christ!

Obstacles to a Clear Vision

Expectations

How do the expectations of others affect the way we live our lives? Can we or should we live up to them? Do they help us see what God had in mind for us or cloud that vision? What about our own expectations? Do they get in the way of discovering our real purpose in life?

As a football coach, I was often aware that some of the dads of players were putting a lot of pressure on their sons to perform at a very high level. I was suspicious that this was more about the parent's ego than wishing the best for their child. I have seen similar behaviors from parents who are the same way about getting their child into the "right schools" and the "right career."

As you can imagine, I have seen a variety of responses from the kids. Sometimes it is outright rebellion, sometimes it is the more subtle, passive-aggressive response and sometimes it is grudging compliance. Maybe the saddest response is that the kid will totally "buy in" to the parent's expectations and "bury" his or her own dreams and goals.

On the other hand, parent's expectations can be positive. My own father always told me that I was smart and that his wish for me was to learn a skill that that would enable me to "be better off" than he, an unskilled laborer.

As an immigrant from Norway, with little formal education, he felt that was his lot. (I have since learned that this is typical of immigrant parents. Not realizing the American Dream for themselves, they urge their kids to achieve it.) Fortunately, he encouraged me to find my own career niche and follow the dreams of my own choosing.

Parents should not be sculpting their children into their own image. We are made in God's image, so the question is. . . What did God have in mind when he formed your child?

To be really free to discover your own purpose means having the will to examine the expectations that you live by and evaluate whose they are. It means asking God to help you discern how He has created you and what purpose he has in mind for you.

Exceeding Expectations

Jared was a third string slot receiver. He had an amazing attitude and an exceptional work ethic. He was small and not very fast.

He did not get into the varsity games but was an enthusiastic supporter from the sidelines.

One game, near the season end, we had a comfortable lead. My offensive coordinator came to me near the end of the game and suggested we get Jared in the game and let him get the ball.

I readily agreed but was concerned that a pass play at this time might be construed as "running up the score." We were a long way from the end zone and thought "Oh well, we'll call a little screen pass that won't amount to too much."
You could see how excited he was when the play was called. He caught the ball, dodged a tackler, then another. He was suddenly in the open field with a two defenders converging on him at about the five-yard line. At this point the whole team and coaching staff are screaming, "Go Jared!" He then launches himself toward the goal line. The defenders dive toward him. And miss! He lands in the end zone! The sideline erupted! When the game ended, the opposing coach understood and was very gracious.

We all are guilty of laying on of expectations that are not accurate; on others as well as on ourselves. We must see ourselves (and others) as God sees us. His expectations can only be realistic!

Expectations: God's Requirements!

What are God's expectations for our lives? Wouldn't those be much harder to live up to than our parents' expectations (or our own faulty ones)?

> *"O people, the Lord has told you what is good,and this is what he requires of you: to do what is right, to love mercy,and to walk humbly with your God." Micah 6:8 (NLT)*

Well, how are we doing with those requirements? On the surface, we may feel we are doing enough. After all, I do my best to treat people well and I have compassion for others and I even do my daily devotions.

Then we come across the Sermon on the Mount in Matthew 5 through 7. Here Jesus sets the bar to a seemingly impossible height.

It's not just murder that you have to answer for; its hate!
It's not just adultery; it's lusting!
It's turn the other cheek and love your enemies!

"You can enter God's Kingdom only through the narrow gate. The highway to hell is broad, and its gate is wide for the many who choose that way. But the gateway to life is very narrow and the road is difficult, and only a few ever find it."
Matthew 7:13 - 14 (NLT)

Who can live up to those expectations?
On what basis then is our hope?

In Luke 1:37, Mary the mother of Jesus is told;

"For nothing is impossible with God."

The apostle Paul says in Philippians 4:13 (NIV);

"For I can do everything through Christ, who gives me strength."

I believe that God will never ask us to do anything that, with His help, we are not capable of doing. It is through our weakness that He is glorified. It is through Christ that we are strengthened and purified.

Vision Requires Action

"Vision without execution is just hallucination." – Henry Ford

I had a counseling session once with a young man who was failing his classes in eighth grade. He explained that grades didn't matter to him because he was going to be a professional basketball player and thus a millionaire. I then asked him how much time each day he spent practicing. He replied "about a half hour a day." When I pointed out that it would take way more than that, and that he needed good grades to be eligible to play at school, he denied that this was so and left my office.

His dream was not accompanied by the work required to accomplish it. I also believe that, in his world, there was no support system to embrace him, give him a realistic vision of who God created him to be or to inspire him to work toward any goal whatsoever. These were real obstacles for him.

Sometimes we cannot see because we have become "victims" of our situation. However, there are countless "victims" who have overcome their situations to live amazing lives of purpose. The Biblical Joseph overcame slavery, false accusations and imprisonment to become a powerful leader and rescue his people from starvation.

Abe Lincoln overcame poverty to become the President of the United States. Jackie Robinson overcame prejudice to become the first black man to play baseball in the modern major leagues. Nick Vujicic has no arms or legs; yet today he is an amazing inspirational speaker. Russell Wilson was considered too short for the National Football League. He is now the quarterback of the Super-bowl champion Seattle Seahawks. All of them have realized their dreams and inspired others to overcome whatever circumstances life has given them.

As a teacher and coach, I was most frustrated with students and athletes who did not work to achieve their potential. Many lacked the self-esteem to realize their own talent.

The effect of these athletes' attitudes not only affected their personal performance, but affected of the team's performance as well. As a coach, it was my job to help them see (envision) what they were really capable of achieving.

Don James, legendary University of Washington football coach, once told me that what he was looking for in recruiting high school players was for them to dominate their opponents on the field. After that, I passed this on to my players, especially those who had NCAA Division I potential.

The message was, "it is not good enough to just defeat your opponent, you need to dominate him." This vision of domination not only affected their individual performance, it significantly improved our team's performance. We all need to heed the advice of Coach James. Are we really doing the best job possible or are we just getting by with an adequate performance? With God's help, we can move from adequacy to excellence!

Without a vision that challenges our poor self-image, individual and group performances never reach potential. Abraham Maslow and Michelangelo both see this as holding individuals and mankind back.

> "The story of the human race is the story of men and women selling themselves short" Abraham Maslow
> "If you deliberately plan to be less than you are capable of being, then I want you to know that you will be deeply unhappy for the rest of your life." A. Maslow
>
> "The greater danger for most men lies not in setting their aim too high and falling short, but in setting our aim too short and achieving our mark." Michelangelo

Many times our vision of ourselves is limited to <u>who we are now</u>. We need to challenge ourselves and others to get hold of a vision of <u>who we could be.</u>

Many years after he had graduated, I had a former student tell me that, "You saw something in me that I could not see myself. Because you pointed it out to me, I came to see it myself; and that has made a huge difference in who I am today."

Can we show (envision) young people to see themselves in a positive light? Yes; with God's help!

The Ability to See.

How do we see God's presence in our lives? Is He only there when we are praying or worshiping. Do we really believe that he is omnipresent, always here?
Perhaps we see God only when we are in dire need of Him (God the Cosmic Vending Machine). And if he doesn't respond like we hope, do we feel abandoned and alone. We don't feel or see His presence.

Brother Lawrence, A 17TH century lay kitchen worker in a French monastery, is noted for his ideas on, "Practicing the Presence of God." His thoughts on this were later written down into a small, but thought-provoking, book by that title. He emphasized that one could realize that God was present as he loved Him through his work. Brother Lawrence, the kitchen worker, referred to himself as the "Lord of Pots and Pans."

Focus, Paying Attention and Peripheral Vision

To better respond to our omnipresent God, a look at some "vision" words might help. The first of these is to "focus." It means to adjust our sight to a point of clarity and sharpness of vision. To mentally focus is to narrow our thoughts on a particular idea or person; to eliminate or reduce outside distractions. In prayer and worship, God becomes our focus.

Some people come by this naturally. I am one. I can literally get lost in a book or project that I am working on.
This has sometimes brought consternation from my wife and daughters. When my kids were teens, they would try to get my attention with; "Dad." "Dad." "DAD!" All this was to no avail. Finally they would say, "Mr. Erickson." They knew, that as a teacher, I would always respond to that.

Another is to "pay attention." Sometimes we use these words to mean to focus. As a classroom teacher or a parent we ask our kids to "pay attention" when what we really mean is to "focus" on what we are sharing at the moment. Paying attention means taking it all in. It is very different than focusing. The idea is to see the whole picture. To see all that is going on around you.

God is not only in a beautiful sunset but also in the daily chores of our lives. In this sense, Brother Lawrence knew that God was there with him always. As a response to this knowledge, He saw and responded to God in his kitchen as he worked.

Paying attention to God, practicing His presence, is the catalyst for growing closer in our relationship with God. This opens our mind to see what God's will is for our lives.

Do we see God in our daily life and work? It is not a question of "Is He there?" The question is "Am I paying enough attention to the fact that He is?" Sometimes we are so "focused" on the task at hand that we are oblivious to God's presence all around us. Now the question is, do we see God in the daily life of the kids we work with? Can we help them to see that?

As a football coach, I have noticed that the better players all had great "peripheral vision". They could see things on the edges better. They had a bigger picture of things going on around them. This helped them recognize both danger (they didn't get blindsided) and opportunities (they could see where they needed to be).

To envision all of who God is and what He has planned for our lives, we need to learn to see in three different ways.

1. We need to be able to **focus** in prayer and worship.
2. We need to **pay attention** to the big picture of God in our lives.
3. We need to work on expanding our **peripheral vision** to see a wider view of what God is up to.

Questions to Ponder

Is there a need for the young person to focus on God right now?
Is there a need for the young person to pay attention to God's presence in their environment?
Is there a need for the young person to use peripheral vision to get a bigger picture of God at work?

A Vision Strategy

Once you have embraced someone, showed them through your love that they indeed have value, they become open to your teaching and open to "seeing" what they have been created to do.

Teach them to focus, pay attention and develop peripheral vision.

Being able to **focus** on a specific topic or person,

paying attention to the big picture and developing peripheral vision are critical to understanding your life's purpose.

Being able to focus is a skill that can be learned. It can be fairly easy to focus on something you are passionate about, but harder to focus on something not so interesting to you.

Have young people look for details and specifics

In a Bible study, you search the few verses that pertain to a particular topic. The same is true for other topics of interest. I have taken classes on specific topics such as digital photography or life coaching. As a football coach, I always had a portion of practice where we worked on fundamental skills, like form tackling, running crisp pass routes and blocking techniques. The details do matter.

These details help build habits and thought patterns that give us the efficiency and information we need.

Taking children into the outdoors with a magnifying glass can open a whole new view of God's creation. Focus helps us see God in the details of life.

Have them eliminate distractions

Trying to go deeper with a subject or a relationship is difficult in a crowded room. Crowded can mean not only too many people but also too much noise, too much movement or perhaps too many text or phone messages. Find a place with silence and solitude to really focus well. This is hard for those of us who are tied to our technology. Noise is our constant companion and we are in perpetual communication with our "peeps." Silence and solitude can be very uncomfortable for some, and a shock to others.

Have them start small and grow

In the beginning, it is best to focus for short periods of time. As you get better at it, you will get lost in it and lose track of the time. That is a sign you have honed the skill of focusing.

As a youth leader, I would introduce silence and solitude on retreats. I would ask kids to find a place, in a natural setting, to spend time with God. They were to be alone with no technology. I would give them a Bible verse, a few open ended questions, and tell them to ask God to speak to them in that place.

Then just listen and observe for about 20 minutes. My small group leaders would then spend another 20 minutes helping them to reflect on the experience. We called this our "Holy Ground" time. The first time I tried this, I wondered how the kids would respond. My worries ended when one of the girls in the group insisted in guiding her dad across an open field to see her "Holy Ground" when he picked her up at the conclusion of the camp.

Paying attention is also a skill that can be learned. You have heard it said we sometimes "can't see the forest for the trees." We can't let the details obscure the big picture in work, in relationships, or in our life purpose.

Help them get an overview

As a teacher, I would ask kids to do a "Natural Geographic" for any new material we were starting to cover. That means to skim the material by looking at the pictures, graphs, maps or charts and read the captions under each.
The idea is to get some ideas of what was important in the material. What is the point, goal, scope and purpose of this? Is there a big message? Reading the introductions, the first and last chapters, and the bold type also give clues to the big picture of a book. Commentaries and summaries by others are also important in getting this big picture.

Have them explore their world

Youth need to understand the big picture of Christianity. Too often they (and we) see our faith only through the eyes of our own particular church or denomination. Reading a book or article by fellow Christians can give us a broader picture of our faith. I have found that Philip Yancey, Richard Foster, Henri Nouwen, and C. S. Lewis have given me a better understanding of my own faith. I then try to read the authors that they frequently refer to in their books. Early Christian writers like St. Augustine, Thomas a Kempis, St. Francis, St. John of the Cross and Brother Lawrence help us to see how God has guided people for two thousand years.

As a teacher, counselor, coach and youth pastor, I went to workshops and clinics to learn new things about my profession. Encourage them to learn more. Be curious.

Have them search the past and scan the horizon

The past gives us clues to who we are. This is true for us as individuals, as Christians, as citizens of a country, as members of a culture and as a resident in our world. Knowing history helps us understand not only the present but the trends that lead us into the future.

As a coach, my game plan (for the current week) was based on the scouting report (what the other team has done in the past). A good coach also scouts his own team. Reflection on our own past is valuable in planning ahead.

Taking a look down the road helps us to see a danger or an opportunity that may lie in our path. As a student, it is critical to know when a test is coming.

Our look at the life ahead helps us to be ready for those known milestones (graduation, marriage, children, or retirement) as well as "pop quizzes" in life (accidents, illnesses, or layoffs).

As we look ahead, it is important to examine our dreams and desires. The big question here is . . . Is this dream or desire part of Gods will?
I believe that these can be from God, but some serious evaluation is needed to eliminate any selfish motives. With prayer, reflection, the guidance of mature Christian mentors and patience, God will reveal his will.

Peripheral vision can also be developed. Even if we pay attention to our portion of the world, it is always good to expand that view to other possible worlds out there. Our personal worlds can sometimes be narrow. We don't have to be "narrow minded."

One Sunday, I was teaching a lesson to seventh and eighth graders. We were discussing how struggles in life could strengthen us. I had each student share a personal experience with a struggle. After a few kids had shared, we came to a seventh grade girl who I knew was adopted out of an orphanage in Guatemala. I asked her if she would share her story. The class sat quietly as she shared that at age five she had lost her mother who died giving birth to her younger brother. Her father then sold the baby and abandoned the family. She and her five older sisters were given to various family members. She suffered abuse from an uncle and ran away to the streets. She ended up in a Christian orphanage and from there was adopted by a family in our community. The rest of the class was unable to share any more of their struggles. In comparison to her story, their troubles seemed of no consequence. Their peripheral vision of life had just been expanded.

Encourage youth to explore other points of view

Some people don't realize the varying ideas that exist within Christianity.
 This is true also in political parties, music, art, and many other aspects of our life.

Read the classics (Voltaire, Socrates, St. Augustine, or C.S. Lewis). Read both the conservative and the liberal. Read not to be converted, but to widen your understanding. You may find that as your perspective is widened, your values and faith are strengthened.

If you look and explore, you may find some really good stuff that broadens your view. The point here is to keep and nourish your curiosity in an amazing world. Seek God in His whole creation!

Encourage them to love and serve the poor, the widow, and the unlovable

This should start in your own community. Then expand to your own country, and then the world. You will discover what God is up to in areas you hadn't thought of before. But the greatest discovery will likely be about who you really are.

God calls us to love our neighbor. He does not qualify this by saying the neighbor must be a nice person. Loving people with whom we don't agree or vary in any way from our "normal" can be uncomfortable, difficult, or even painful. This will take courage. We can only do this with God's help. He will bless us for it.

To be able to focus, to pay attention, and to use our peripheral vision all help to envision what the Kingdom of God is about. We learn who God is and what he is up to. We discover that we are made for a purpose. That purpose, when realized, brings others to God's Kingdom.

The Ultimate Vision Strategy

As much as we think we understand who Jesus was and is, we always come up short. Our peripheral vision just isn't wide enough. We can find comfort in the disciple Peter. In Mark 8, Peter declares Jesus the Messiah. Then in the next moment, he totally misunderstands what Messiah means. We must reflect on this and listen. **God is always bigger than you think**. Through His Holy Spirit, He will continually show us more of who He is.

> "For now we see only a reflection as in a mirror; then *we shall see face to face. Now I know in part; then I shall know fully, even as I am fully known."* 1 Corinthians 13:12 (NIV)

Teach them who God is and what his Kingdom is about

This is a lifelong process. Prayer, Bible study, sermons, and books all help to grasp how big our God is.

To keep from putting God in a box, we need to constantly remind ourselves that we cannot define Him completely. However, we can understand Him more today than we did yesterday. Asking for help from the Holy Spirit and other Spirit-led people can guide us to a deepening truth.

It is important to teach that reflection (on what you have read or heard or experienced) is critical to learning. Three questions help one to pause and think about the study and/or experience.

The three questions are;

What? (What specifically is said? Who is speaking? To Whom? Where is this taking place? When? What happened?)

So What? (So what does it mean? Put into your own words.)

Now What? (So what do I do? How do I best put this into action?)

This reflective tool provides the framework for learning and changing directions.

Share Your Story!

Perhaps the best way to teach about God is to share your faith story.

Describe how you have grown, how you have failed and how you have been forgiven. How did you learn about your skills, passions, and dreams? How has your experience and your relationship with God grown your faith? The most effective witness to others is the Gospel according to "you."

Teach them that, once you have trusted God with your salvation, God begins to change your character.

This, like knowing God and His Kingdom, is a lifelong process. The churchy word for this is "sanctification." Max Lucado, in his book *Just Like Jesus*, says that "God loves you just the way you are but he refuses to leave you that way." Through the Holy Spirit, God moves into your life and starts renovation. As He tears out this wall or adds a window there, His goal is to make you more and more like Himself.

Character

It has been said that God is more concerned about our character than our comfort. How is it then that God develops our character?

> *"Not only so, but we also glory in our sufferings, because we know that suffering produces perseverance; perseverance, character; and character, hope." Romans 5:3-4 (NIV)*

"Consider it pure joy, my brothers and sisters, whenever you face trials of many kinds, because you know that the testing of your faith produces perseverance. Let perseverance finish its work so that you may be mature and complete, not lacking anything." James 1:2-4 (NIV)

He gives us suffering and trials? Don't these experiences tear us down? If you look closely at the above passages, two phrases stand out: "glory in our suffering" and "Consider it pure joy." These instructions pertain to our **attitude** while in a difficult situation. (Note: Happiness or unhappiness is a feeling based on the circumstances we are in, while to glory or to consider joy are an attitude that we choose no matter our circumstances.)

For many summers now, I have taken kids to Camp Bighorn in western Montana. The camp puts kids in what they call the **adventure zone**. It takes them out of their **comfort zone** but never lets them get into a **danger zone**. The camp does this through both individual and group initiatives. Individually, this is achieved through rock climbing, mountain biking, river kayaking, white water rafting and a high ropes course that ends with a zip line ride.

The group initiatives involve group problem solving and building trust. "Huck Finn" has them build a raft that will actually float their group on a river. A low ropes course challenges them to rely on each other to overcome obstacles.

The reasoning behind these adventures is to put kids in a situation where they must decide which character traits to display: joy, perseverance, courage, and humility. They also choose to encourage each other, to build each other up, to listen with empathy and inspire by example.

God uses the everyday situations we live through to give us an opportunity to grow in character. What is the difference between our sufferings defeating us or building our character? The difference is choosing to believe that God is there for us no matter what. When we "glory in" or "consider it joy," we trust God and his promise of hope.

This process gives us hope for our future. In Hebrews 11:1, Paul, the Apostle, describes this hope.

> "Now faith is being sure of what we hope for and certain of what we do not see." (NIV)

Author Jim Wallis paraphrases this by saying,

"Hope means believing in spite of the evidence, then watching the evidence change."

Step Programs

A really great tool that can help change us is a Step program.
Alcoholics Anonymous, Celebrate Recovery, and other 12 step programs can provide a structure and the support to help a person grow and change. The 12 steps address reliance on God, a self-inventory, confession, making amends, and helping others. God has used these to help "sanctify" many people. Celebrate Recovery is available in many churches and Alcoholics/Narcotics Anonymous is available in most communities. Journey to Freedom is a 12 step program offered at many YMCA's. I have used the Celebrate Recovery youth curriculum called *the Landing* to help young people grow and mature in their faith and their character.

A word of caution about building character

"Do not be misled: 'Bad company corrupts good character.'" 1 Corinthians 15:33 (NIV)

As a counselor and youth pastor, I have told my charges the there is a big difference between having friends and being friendly. I believe we are required to be friendly to all. (Love thy neighbor!) I also believe if we want to grow in Christian character then we need to choose our friends wisely. This doesn't mean to have only Christians as friends, but to look for friends that display solid positive character. Remind the young that it is not the number of friends you have but the quality of each friendship.

Wisdom

To help us understand sanctification, God offers us an amazing tool: wisdom. God was pleased in the Old Testament when King Solomon chose the gift of wisdom over the gifts of power and riches. This gift is offered to each of us as well.

> *"If any of you lacks wisdom, you should ask God, who gives generously to all without finding fault, and it will be given to you. But when you ask, you must believe and not doubt," James 1:5-6(NIV)*

As we work with the next generation we must ask for wisdom for ourselves and encourage them to ask for godly wisdom for themselves.

Fruits of the Spirit

Any discussion of character would not be complete without mentioning the work of the Holy Spirit. As we grow spiritually, as we cooperate with the Holy Spirit in the battle with our sinful desires, certain character traits will begin to show up in our lives.

> *"But the fruit of the Spirit is love, joy, peace, forbearance, kindness, goodness, faithfulness, gentleness and self-control. Against such things there is no law. Those who belong to Christ Jesus have crucified the flesh with its passions and desires. Since we live by the Spirit, let us keep in step with the Spirit." Galatians 5:22-25 (NIV)*

These "fruits" can be the subject of our prayer life. Encourage the next generation to seek these character traits as they pray and grow. Pick a "fruit of the month" to focus those prayers and watch what God will do.

Help them discover who they are created to be and do. ("You are God's masterpiece, created to do the works He has planned for you to do.")

As you embrace them, notice their skills, talents, Spiritual Gifts, personality type, and their passions. Point out things you have noticed. Encourage them to take Spiritual Gift inventories and personality tests. Follow these surveys up with reflective discussions. (What? So what? Now what?)

Ask them questions about their experiences, passions and dreams. Resist the temptation to tell them the path to take, even if they ask you. You can, however, share what traits, talents, gifts that you see in them. This can be important information, especially if they had not been aware of it. Just the other day, I was a substitute teacher in a classroom. I pointed out to a young man that he had a "radio" voice. It was deep and resonating and words sort of just "rolled" out of his mouth smoothly. This was new information to him. He smiled and said he would have to think about that. A seed was planted!

Sometimes a seed planted can send a young person on a journey that you have not anticipated. I once told one of my graduating football players that he should consider a dance class to help with his balance and footwork for his quest to play community college football. The next time I saw him was a couple of years later when he performed at our high school with a dance troupe. His football future had become a dance career.

This process must be their discovery, their journey. Trust that God will speak to them. Encourage them to listen to God. Remind them that God has given them the tools to accomplish His purpose for their lives. Pray with them and for them.

Remind them that they are chosen by God to change the world. Encourage them to get involved in serving others. Brainstorm possibilities for this. Help them reflect on these experiences. (What happened? What did they learn? What to do next?) Each little step on this journey is important for learning one's place in God's kingdom.

I have used several workbooks to take young people through a process that will help them discover who they are and how that can show them what their life purpose is.

Tony Stoltzfus has written *A Leader's Life Purpose* workbook. It is excellent for one on one mentoring. C. Gene Wilkes' *Jesus on Leadership* is also helpful. For teen parents, *How Your Teenager is Wired* by Katie Brazelton is really good. There is a companion student devotional *The Way I'm Wired* for the teen who is motivated to really go deeper. Also check out *S.H.A.P.E.* by Eric Rees.

Teach them that clarity of vision comes in steps.

> *"They came to Bethsaida, and some people brought a blind man and begged Jesus to touch him. He took the blind man by the hand and led him outside the village. When he had spit on the man's eyes and put his hands on him, Jesus asked, "Do you see anything?" He looked up and said, "I see people; they look like trees walking around." Once more Jesus put his hands on the man's eyes. Then his eyes were opened, his sight was restored, and he saw everything clearly." Mark 8:22-25 (NIV)*

The blind man wasn't healed the first time that Jesus touched him. Our journey with God takes time.

Even though I was teaching, coaching, and counseling for a long time, my purpose (to embrace, envision, and inspire the next generation) was not clear until I was 25 years into my career.

To put this into a book, came 15 years after that. That's what happened to Joseph in the Bible. He had a vision experience at about age 17. It did not come to fruition until he was in his late thirties. I recommend Tony Stoltzfus' book *The Calling Journey* to really understand this lifetime process.

"For now we see only a reflection as in a mirror; then we shall see face to face. Now I know in part; then I shall know fully, even as I am fully known." 1 Corinthians 13:12

Conclusion

To envision is to help someone see who he or she is in Christ. It is a process that takes time, reflection, prayer, and perseverance. For the next generation to really see their life purpose, they must first be embraced. Embracing gives you credibility with them.

Credibility gives you the opportunity to help open their eyes to see what God has created them to do. As you embrace these young people and help them envision a purposeful life, you will need to inspire them through encouragement and through your example.

To Inspire

"Then the Lord God formed a man from the dust of the ground and breathed into his nostrils the breath of life, and the man became a living being."
Genesis 2:7 (NIV)

Tell them they are chosen by inspiring them on their journey!

As I write this I am thinking of my friend, Rick, who passed away yesterday (October 14, 2013) from cancer. Rick was a fierce fighter. In late July, I had lunch with him and he was passionately planning to get more involved in the care of those suffering from mental illness. He was the first "peer counselor" in our town. A peer counselor is one who has himself been a mental illness patient and is now counseling those who also struggle with those issues.

Our lunch conversation was difficult because his cancer had taken away most of his hearing. He read lips, read my responses generated through Dragon speech on my ipad, and asked for clarifications. Mostly I listened as he shared his passion for what he wanted to accomplish for those who are lost and confused.

Rick had an amazing love for God, his wife, and his son and daughter. The closer he came to his life's end, the closer he acted on his core values. He willingly showed others the effects of the cancer. By September, he was totally blind, deaf, and unable to walk. His speech was very slurred. There is an amazing video on YouTube of him baptizing his young daughter. His sharing of the gospel and his hopes for the faith of his children is so touching that it is life changing. His life of faith inspired his kids to make it their own.

Rick showed that inspiration comes from overcoming. We are moved to action when we see people accomplish something beyond their real, or imagined, limitations. We are at first surprised; then inspired. They don't always have to accomplish the task. We can be inspired by valiant effort. Inspiration can come from a courageous fight in a "losing" battle.

Rick's legacy lives on in his family and friends. This June (2014) Rick's son was awarded two inspirational awards at his school, one for orchestra and one for ninth grade leadership. Inspired people inspire others!

Definitions

To inspire literally means to "breathe into" to "give life to." It is about helping others to succeed. It motivates others to accomplish. It goes deeper than logic.

Simon Sineck in his book, *Start with Why: How Great Leaders Inspire Everyone to Take Action*, explains that this is part of our biology. Our outer brain is where our logic and language reside. This outer brain surrounds our inner brain levels where our "how" and deeper yet, our "why" functions reside. He says to effectively motivate or inspire we must appeal to these inner levels where our values and feelings are stored. These inner reaches of our brain have no language. They are affected most by seeing, hearing and feeling.

That is why people's stories, real or fiction, inspire us more than logic. Logic may persuade the mind (outer brain) but inspiration will persuade the heart (inner brain). Inspiration reaches deeper and is the most effective motivator.

The heart's passion will trump the persuasion of logic. That said, passion might need to be tempered by logic (Truth sets us free). An inspirational example of rational thinking may be in order. A person who has "overcome" this issue may "speak to the heart" of others. That example must reach the "heart" of the listener to be effective.

My pastor for most of my life used to say that Christianity must be "caught" more than "taught." My faith and values were "caught" from my parents, teachers, coaches, and pastors. As informational as these mentors were, what I saw in their lives was the motivation to become who I am today. Their words were effective, but the lives behind them gave those words their power.

As a football player, the older players whose enthusiasm and example led me to play harder influenced me the most. I wanted to be like them. I, too, played with that passion. I was never the most talented player on the team, but I worked hard, was focused and became a technician at my position. My work ethic and my enthusiasm were recognized by teammates. I was honored to win the Inspirational Award in both high school and in college.

Inspiration speaks to the heart, it motivates, it spurs others to action, and it provides an example. It is emotional.

It expresses our deepest values in a way that reaches deep into the heart of others. It is the projection of values and emotion that give you role model status.

Skill and talent may set the stage for your performance, but your expression of values and emotion on that stage is the inspiration.

One of my fondest memories from my coaching days is the story of Billie. Billie was small and slow, but he loved football. He loved the game and he loved being on a team. He loved his teammates and admired their talent. At the season ending awards banquet, I always told my players that the Inspirational Award is the highest award you could win. After Billie's junior year banquet he asked me if that award had to go to a "starter." I said that it always had in the past, but that was not a requirement. He then told me that he was going to win it his senior year.

The next fall, Billie started campaigning for the Inspirational Award. He told the players and the coaches that he was going to be this year's winner. Billie never started a varsity game. However, he was always first in line for every drill, he shouted encouragement to his teammates from the sideline of every game. He celebrated each victory and was uplifting and encouraging in each loss.

During our rival game, he was especially vocal and enthusiastic. After winning the game, we were still celebrating in our locker room. One of our players came to get me and said that something was wrong with Billie. I sat him down in the coaches' office and discovered that he was hyperventilating. We had him breath into a paper bag. He was soon fine but exhausted. He had not played a down of offense or defense in the game, yet he had given everything he had for the team. With a landslide vote of his teammates, Billie won the Inspirational Award for his senior year.

Examples of inspiration can come at an early age. At about eight or nine years old (1955-56), I was on our elementary school playground. A boy was choosing between two other boys for some reason that I can't remember. He said, "Eeeny Meeny Miny Moe, catch an n-word by the toe."
Just then, a young black girl tapped him on the shoulder from behind. She did not say a word. She just looked at him. He turned red and ran off. I remember that incident clearly even though it was nearly 60 years ago. Whenever I have seen people stand up for what is right in this world, I think of her. What an inspiring example of courage and strong self-esteem!

I have been privileged to have coaches who have been inspirational to me. In high school, my head coach had a strict rule of no swearing on the field.

If you slipped up, you had to run a lap around our practice field. One day, he became frustrated with one of our players who didn't want to do what the coach was asking him to do. Out came the word, "Dammit." The next day, without explaining, coach ran a lap before practice. We all knew the reason. His integrity was inspiring!

The Strategy

As we have embraced the next generation, and helped them to see their God given purpose we need to inspire them on their journey.

We can all be an inspiration to others. The Bible calls us to "build each other up," to "encourage one another," and to "spur each other on."

Encourage them

Be a cheerleader in their lives. Words can build up or tear down. Be positive. Great job! Way to go! Go for it! I know you can! Yes! This needs to be done with enthusiasm. I am a yeller. Kids have told me that they can hear me above the crowd noise when I am a hundred yards away. Be passionate about their wins and when they have a setback, be passionate in your assurance that they can overcome.

Come alongside those who are struggling. Be careful not to tell them their pain is no big thing. Recognize their pain and offer prayer and a listening ear. Your compassionate presence is itself the biggest encouragement.

Be an example. Take the initiative to act.

Be the "first in line." This is about being there. It is hard, but not impossible. Even if you are not a yeller, like I am, your presence is a big encouragement. Encourage even when you are not present with them. A quick text message or an old-school phone call can mean a lot to a struggling teen.

Your character counts big time!

Your humility is a great example (Sometimes you need to be "last in line" or not on first string). Forgiveness and reconciliation, coming from you, send a great message.
Nelson Mandela was a great inspiration to the whole world because of his refusal to "get even" when he had the chance.

Celebrate their success!

Your joy in their accomplishment can lead to even more accomplishment. A party, a card sent, a text or email congratulations all serve to inspire. Your enthusiasm tells them they are chosen!

Your story can be an inspiration.

Share your faith. How have you struggled? How have you overcome? How has God guided your journey? Describe your successes and failures? Ask them about their story. Listen. Have more questions than answers, about their story and yours. Talk and ask about dreams.

Conclusion

People are motived by actions more than arguments; dreams more than plans; ideas more than facts. Your example is louder that your words; though words, if positive, can have great effect. Your enthusiasm and passion have power beyond reason. To inspire is to give life to another.

Going Deeper

"I pray that out of his glorious riches he may strengthen you with power through his Spirit in your inner being, so that Christ may dwell in your hearts through faith. And I pray that you, being rooted and established in love, may have power, together with all the Lord's holy people, to grasp how wide and long and high and deep is the love of Christ, and to know this love that surpasses knowledge—that you may be filled to the measure of all the fullness of God." Ephesians 3:16-19 (NIV)

This book is about developing relationships with young people. It is about going the extra mile, to not only tell them they are chosen but to show them they are chosen. I have included, in chapter 6, a series of topics, experiences and resources that I hope you can use to bring a deeper understanding of embracing someone and guiding them to envision their life purpose.

Each topic has a **Read it** heading that usually includes Bible passages that speak to the topic.

That is followed by a **Discuss it** heading that asks for some reflective thinking. **These questions are best when used in a small group but can be an individual devotion.**

Each topic then has a **Pray it** section that is specific to that subject.

Finally, there is a **Challenge** heading to apply this topic in a personal way.

The video clips are from the Wing Clips web site. (http://www.wingclips.com) Most can be viewed for free from your computer.

At the end of these 26 topics, I have included some **resources** that were foundational to this book and great reading for anyone who is committed to helping young people discover God's purpose for their lives.

Topic 1 – God *knows me*!

Read it . . . Genesis 1:26-28, 31, Psalm 139 -1-12, 13-16, John 10:3, Matthew 10:30, Job 14:16, Psalm 56:8, Psalm 3:23, John 14:20

Discuss it . . . When I realize that God knows me I . . .

Pray it . . . Spend 2 minutes in silence asking God to show me who I am.

Challenge . . . to <u>pray each day</u> for God to show them someone who needs to be blessed by them.

Topic 2 – You Are _Chosen_ by God!!

Video clips -
Letters to God – **"God chose you to be my mom!"**
The Shine of Rainbows – **"Why did you choose me?"**
Narnia The Voyage of the Dawn Trader – **"You have a destiny!"**

Read it . . . God has chosen me!
Jeremiah 1:4-10, John 15:16, Ephesians 1:4, Mark 13:20, Luke 18:7, Acts 22:14, Colossians 3:12, 1 Thessalonians 1:4,
1 Peter 2:9

Discuss it . . .
Opening Question – I would like to be chosen as _____!

1. What is it like to be chosen to do something fun?
2. What is it like to be chosen to do something hard?
3. What is it like to be chosen first when picking teams?
4. What is it like to be chosen last when picking teams?
5. How would you feel if you got a clear message from God (like Jeremiah) to be God's "mouthpiece"?
6. What does Acts 22:14 say about being chosen?
7. What would you like God to choose you to do? Is that likely?
8. What does Colossians 3:12 ask you to

do as a "chosen" person? How might you do that at your school?

9. Read 1 Peter 2:9. Who are you? Who's your daddy?

Pray it . . . Spend 2 minutes in silence asking God to help you feel "chosen."

Challenge . . . to pray each day for God to show you someone who needs to be chosen by you.

Topic 3 - God made me to be me!

Video clip – *Thunderpants* –"A fruit from God"

Read it . . .
Ephesians 2:10 (NLT)
For we are God's masterpiece (poiema = poem).
He has created us anew in Christ Jesus, so we can
do the good things he planned for us long ago.

Romans 12:4-8 (MSG)
Each of us finds our meaning and function as a
part of his body. But as a chopped-off finger or
cut-off toe we wouldn't amount to much, would
we? . . . let's just go ahead and be what we were
made to be, without enviously or pride fully
comparing ourselves with each other, or trying
to be something we aren't.

1 Corinthians 12:14-18 (MSG)
I want you to think about how all this makes you
more significant, not less.

As it is, we see that God has carefully placed each
part of the body right where he wanted it.

1 Corinthians 27-31 (MSG)
You are Christ's body—that's who you are! You
must never forget this.

1 Corinthians 13:1-3 (NLT) If I could speak all the languages of earth and of angels, but didn't love others, I would only be a noisy gong or a clanging cymbal. If I had the gift of prophecy, and if I understood all of God's secret plans and possessed all knowledge, and if I had such faith that I could move mountains, but didn't love others, I would be nothing. If I gave everything I have to the poor and even sacrificed my body, I could boast about it; but if I didn't love others, I would have gained nothing.

Discuss it . . .

Opening Question – Most people don't know that I . . .

1. Sometimes I wish I could be like . . . (person)
2. Who are your "role models"? (besides Jesus)
3. Who are some positive people to emulate? Some negative people to not emulate?
4. To me "peer pressure" means . . .
5. Have you ever tried to "copy" someone?
6. Have you ever tried to change your "image"? Clothes, hair, behavior?
7. What do you think it means <u>for you</u> to be God's Masterpiece (poem)?
8. What makes you unique (besides fingerprints and DNA)?
9. What does Love have to do with who I am?

Pray it . . . Spend 2 minutes in silence asking God to show you how you are unique.

Challenge . . . to pray each day for God to show them how they are unique.

What am I created to do?

Topic 4 - God has a plan just for me!

Read it . . .
Ephesians 2:10

Video clip – *A Very Tall Person*

Psalm 139:16b
Jeremiah 29:6-7, 10-14

Video clip - *A Second Chance*

Discuss it . . .
Opening Question – When I grow up I want to be . . .

1. I really admire _____ because he/she is obviously where God wants them to be.
2. <u>People</u> say that I am good at . . .?
3. One talent <u>I think</u> I have is . . .
4. List some ways that God could speak to you about your purpose in life.
5. List some ways you could "pay attention" to what God is telling you.
6. How could your talent (#3) translate into changing the world for God?
7. I think I could best serve God by . . .

Pray it . . . Spend 2 minutes in silence asking God <u>to help you "pay attention" to God's direction for your life.</u>

Challenge . . . to <u>pray each day</u> for God to show them their specific life mission.

Topic 5 - Who is driving this car? TRUST!

Video clip – "I'm swimming" – *Walking across Egypt*

Song - Jesus take the Wheel

Read it . . . Trust passages
Psalm 49: 12-13, Isaiah 31:1, 2 Kings 6, John 14:1, Romans 10:11, Romans 15:13

Discuss it . . .
Opening Question – . . . The person I trust most is . . . (other than God)
1. What is trust?
2. How is trust broken? Any personal examples?
3. How does it make you feel when a trust is broken?
4. How is trust built or taught?
5. Why should we trust God?
6. Does God ever "just shove you in over your head"?
7. When is it hard to give up control? Why is it hard?
8. Under what circumstances is it easier to give up control?
9. How do you trust God more? In what areas of your life?

Pray it . . . Spend 2 minutes in silence asking God to teach me to trust Him.

Challenge to <u>pray each day</u> for God to show them how to trust Him more.

Topic 6 - I am Chosen to be Changed - I have been chosen for an extreme makeover!
Brian Duncan song & lyrics – <u>My House</u>

Read it - John 17:23 (NCV), 1 Thessalonians 5:23-24 (NCV), 2 Corinthians 3:18 (NCV), Romans 8:29 (NCV) Colossians 3:10-12 (NCV), Romans 12:1-2(MSG), Galatians 5:19-21 (NCV), Galatians 5:22-23

Discuss it . . .
Opening Question – If I could change one thing about my character it would be . . .
1. What is sanctification?
   Galatians 5:19-21
2. What are some obvious character flaws listed?
3. Which ones are a problem for people you know? For yourself?
   Galatians 5:22-23
4. What are some obvious character positives listed?
5. Which ones are most desirable for you?
6. What do the "sanctification" verses say about what God intends for your character?

Pray it . . . Spend 2 minutes in silence asking God to <u>"remodel" you into a better person.</u>

Challenge . . . to <u>pray each day</u> for God to change them to be more like Jesus.

Topic 7 - How do I cooperate with God on my extreme makeover?

Read it . . . The story of the two wolves

One evening, an old Cherokee told his grandson about a battle that goes on inside people. He said, "My son, the battle is between two wolves inside us all." One is Evil - it is anger, envy, jealousy, sorrow, regret, greed, arrogance, self-pity, guilt, resentment, inferiority, lies, false pride, superiority, and ego. "The other is Good - it is joy, peace, love, hope, serenity, humility, kindness, benevolence, empathy, generosity, truth, compassion and faith."

The grandson thought about it for a minute and then asked his grandfather, "Which wolf wins?" The old Cherokee simply replied, "The one you feed."

Read the following passages to learn how to "feed the Good wolf."

Philippians 4:8, Jeremiah 29:12-14, Matthew 7:7-8, Matthew 6:33, Psalm 139:23-2 (NIV)

Prayer of surrender - "Thy will be done" & "Not my will but yours Lord"

Pray Psalm 139:23-24

Video - Skit Guys (Tommy & Eddie video – *Psalm 139*) See the Skit Guys web site for this many other great skit videos.

Discuss it . . .
Opening Question – . . . I am open to others pointing out my faults. Why or Why not?
Read Psalm 139:23-24 again

1. What is David saying to God in this passage? (in your own words)
2. Are there some things that you would like for God to change in you? Like what?
3. Are there some things that you would like to hang on to for a while longer? (a "pet sin") Like what?
4. What might keep someone (you) from really letting God really make you over?
5. What does it mean to hold someone accountable? See Proverbs 27:17
6. Describe the type of person you could trust as an accountability partner.
7. Are you that type of person?
8. Do you know and trust someone like that?

Pray it . . . Spend 2 minutes in silence asking God "search your heart for any offensive way in you."

Challenge . . . to pray each day for God to show you your character flaws and heal them.

Topic 7 - Ouch! This remodeling hurts!

Read it . . .
Ephesians 2:8-10, Romans 5:1-5,
James 1:2-6 (NIV)

Video -Skit guys - *Chisel*

Discuss it . . .
Opening Question – . . .How are you a
masterpiece?
1. What would you like God to chisel away in
    others?
2. What are the positive results of suffering?
3. What would you like God to chisel away in
    you?
4. Who decides what God chisels away in
    you?
5. What hurts have made you stronger? How
    so?
6. How can I be joyful when life hurts?

Pray it . . . Spend 2 minutes in silence asking God
to give you strength and joy in suffering?

Challenge . . . to stand up and declare that they
are God's masterpieces (like Tommy in the
video)

Topic 8 - **What is required of me O Lord? How can I act justly?**

Read it . . .
Micah 6:8 (NIV)
He has shown you, O mortal, what is good. And what does the LORD require of you? <u>To act justly</u> and to love mercy and to walk humbly with your God.

To act justly . . . (other Bible versions)
> Do what is fair and just to your neighbor.
> To do what is right
> See that justice is done
> You must treat people fairly
> To do justice
> Isaiah 1:15-18 (NIV)
> When you spread out your hands in prayer, I hide my eyes from you; even when you offer many prayers, I am not listening.
> Your hands are full of blood! Wash and make yourselves clean. Take your evil deeds out of my sight; stop doing wrong. Learn to do right; seek justice. Defend the oppressed; Take up the cause of the fatherless; plead the case of the widow.

To love mercy . . . (other Bible versions)
> Be compassionate and loyal in your love,

love kindness and mercy
let mercy be your first concern
love being kind to others
You must love others faithfully

To walk humbly with your God.
    And you must be very careful to live the
    way your God wants you to.

Discuss it . . .
Opening Question – What "breaks your heart"
the most in your world?

1. Describe the worst bullies you have ever
   known.
2. Have you ever been at the mercy of a
   bully? How was that resolved?
   Read Isaiah 1:15-17
3. What does God want from you in this
   passage?
4. How do you "learn to do right?"
5. Who are the oppressed? In the world? In
   our community?
6. How can you "encourage the oppressed?"
   In the world? In our community?
7. How can you defend the fatherless and
   plead the case of the widow?

Pray it . . . Spend 2 minutes in silence asking God
to help them see oppression and take a stand
against it.

Challenge . . . Ask God to show you the hurting people in your life and give you the courage to embrace them.

Topic 9 – To show mercy . . . so what does that look like?

Read it . . .

A group of professional people posed this question to a group of 4 to 8 year-olds, "What does love mean?" The answers they got were broader and deeper than anyone could have imagined.See what you think:

'When my grandmother got arthritis, she couldn't bend over and paint her toenails anymore. So my grandfather does it for her all the time, even when his hands got arthritis too. That's love.' Rebecca- age 8

'When someone loves you, the way they say your name is different. You just know that your name is safe in their mouth.' Billy - age 4

'Love is when a girl puts on perfume and a boy puts on shaving cologne and they go out and smell each other.' Karl - age 5

'Love is when you go out to eat and give somebody most of your French fries without making them give you any of theirs.' Chrissy - age 6

'Love is what makes you smile when you're tired.' Terri - age 4

'Love is when my mommy makes coffee for my daddy and she takes a sip before giving it to him, to make sure the taste is OK.' Danny - age 7

'Love is when you kiss all the time. Then when you get tired of kissing, you still want to be together and you talk more. My Mommy and Daddy are like that. They look gross when they kiss.' Emily - age 8

'Love is what's in the room with you at Christmas if you stop opening presents and listen.' Bobby - age 7 (Wow!)

'If you want to learn to love better, you should start with a friend who you hate.' Nikka - age 6

'Love is when you tell a guy you like his shirt, then he wears it everyday.' Noelle - age 7

'Love is like a little old woman and a little old man who are still friends even after they know each other so well.' Tommy - age 6

'During my piano recital, I was on a stage and I was scared. I looked at all the people watching me and saw my daddy waving and smiling. He was the only one doing that. I wasn't scared anymore.' Cindy - age 8

'My mommy loves me more than anybody. You don't see anyone else kissing me to sleep at night.' Clare - age 6

'Love is when Mommy gives Daddy the best piece of chicken.' Elaine-age 5

'Love is when Mommy sees Daddy smelly and sweaty and still says he is handsomer than Robert Redford.' Chris - age 7

'Love is when your puppy licks your face even after you left him alone all day.' Mary Ann - age 4

'I know my older sister loves me because she gives me all her old clothes and has to go out and buy new ones.' Lauren - age 4

'When you love somebody, your eyelashes go up and down and little stars come out of you.' *(What an image!)* Karen - age 7
'Love is when Mommy sees Daddy on the toilet and she doesn't think it's gross.' Mark - age 6

'You really shouldn't say 'I love you' unless you mean it. But if you mean it, you should say it a lot. People forget.' Jessica - age 8

And the final one: The winner was a four year old child whose next door neighbor was an elderly gentleman who had recently lost his wife.Upon seeing the man cry, the little boy went into the old gentleman's yard, climbed onto his lap, and just sat there. When his mother asked what he had said to the neighbor, the little boy said, "Nothing, I just helped him cry.'

Video clips
Jesus of Nazareth – "Cast the first stone"
To End all Wars – "human beings"
Les Miserables – "Back to God"

Discuss it . . .
Opening Question – I have the most trouble giving mercy to . . .

1. What do Jesus, the prisoner soldier, and the priest have in common?
2. What do the adulteress, the Japanese soldiers and Jean Val Jean have in common?
3. What do you think the adulteress, the Japanese soldiers and Jean Val Jean did after they were shown mercy?
4. Describe a time when you were given mercy. How did you react to it?
5. What does it mean that God "requires" you to give mercy to people? (Micah 6:8)
6. Who in your life does not deserve your mercy? How might they react if you gave it to them anyway?

Pray it . . . Spend 2 minutes in silence asking God to have courage to show mercy to people.

Challenge . . . to give mercy to an undeserving person this week.

Topic 10 - "To walk humbly with your God"

What is Humility? –
"I believe in God and <u>I am not him</u>!"
"It is much better to humble ourselves than to
have God humble us!"

Why Humility – Christ's example!
Video clips –
Get Down by Audio Adrenalin (see You Tube for
both the video and the lyrics)
"Good advice" from <u>Secret of the Cave</u>

Read it . . . Romans 12:3

Discuss it . . .

Opening Question – I am most humble when. .
.

1. What is humility? (Romans 12:3 in your
   own words)
2. What is the world's definition of a "loser?"
3. In the song "Get Down," what does it
   mean by . . .
"To win you've got to come in last place"
"To live your life you've got to lose it"
"And all the losers get a crown"
4. What is "false humility?"
5. Can you have self-confidence and humility
   at the same time?
6. How does God <u>teach</u> us humility? (This is
   a very scary thing to ask God for!)
7. How might God "lift you up" when you are

116

humble?

8. How could you be humble (a loser?) this next week?

Pray it . . . Spend 2 minutes in silence asking God <u>to remind you about humility this week.</u>

Challenge . . . to humble yourself this next week with your family and friends.

Understanding Jesus

Topic 11 - Jesus is God!

Read it . . .
Genesis 1:1-2, 26 (NIV)
In the beginning <u>God created</u> the heavens and the earth. The earth was formless and empty, and darkness covered the deep waters. And the <u>Spirit of God</u> was hovering over the surface of the waters.

 26Then God said, "Let <u>us</u> make man in <u>our</u> image, after <u>our</u> likeness.

Genesis 3:14-15 (NIV)
The LORD God said to the serpent, "Because you have done this, cursed are you above all livestockand above all beasts of the field;on your belly you shall go,and dust you shall eat all the days of your life. will put enmity between you and the woman, and between your offspring and <u>her offspring;he shall bruise your head,and you shall bruise his heel."</u>

Deuteronomy 6:4 (NIV)
Hear, O Israel: The LORD our God, the LORD is one.

Isaiah 53:4-6 (NIV)

Surely he took up our pain and bore our suffering, yet we considered him punished by God, stricken by him, and afflicted. But he was pierced for our transgressions, he was crushed for our iniquities; the punishment that brought us peace was on him, and by his wounds we are healed. We all, like sheep, have gone astray, each of us has turned to our own way; and the LORD has laid on him the iniquity of us all.

John 1:1-3, 14 (NIV)
<u>In the beginning was the Word</u>, and the Word was with God, and the <u>Word was God</u>. He was in the beginning with God. <u>All things were made through him,</u> and without him was not any thing made that was made.

14And the <u>Word became flesh</u> and dwelt among us, and we have seen his glory, glory as of the only Son from the Father, full of grace and truth.

Exodus 3:13-14 (NIV)
Moses said to God, "Suppose I go to the Israelites and say to them, 'The God of your fathers has sent me to you,' and they ask me, 'What is his name?' Then what shall I tell them?" God said to Moses, <u>"I AM WHO I AM</u>. This is what you are to say to the Israelites: '<u>I AM</u> has sent me to you.'"

Mark 14:61-64 (NIV)

But he remained silent and made no answer. Again the high priest asked him, "Are you the Christ, the Son of the Blessed?" And Jesus said, "I am, and you will see the Son of Man seated at the right hand of Power, and coming with the clouds of heaven." And the high priest tore his garments and said, "What further witnesses do we need? You have heard his blasphemy. What is your decision?" And they all condemned him as deserving death.

Discuss it . . .
1. What / Who is the trinity?
2. What promises are in the Old Testament about Jesus?
3. How does John (the Gospel writer) describe Jesus?
4. What was Jesus' purpose here on earth?
5. How does Jesus describe himself?
6. So what does it mean to you that Jesus is God?
7. Now what can you do this week to respond to the idea Jesus is God?

Pray it . . .
Have a moment of silent prayer about God coming to earth for you? (Thanksgiving or Praise)

Challenge . . .
Envision Jesus putting his arm around you as you pray.

Topic 12- Jesus is "fully human"

Read it . . .
He was like us physically.
1. He was born -Luke 1:31; 2:7
2. He had a body made of skin and bones -Luke24:39; Heb. 2:14
3. He grew -Is. 53:2; Luke 2:40, 52
4. He got hungry -Matt. 4:2; 21:18; Mark 11:12
5. He got thirsty -John 19:28
6. He got tired and slept -Matt. 8:24; John 4:6

He was like us emotionally.
1. He got angry -Matt. 21:12
2. He was betrayed -Matt. 26:14-16; 48-49
3. He was made fun of -Matt. 9:24b; Luke 22:63-65
4. He cried Heb. 5:7; John 11:35; Luke 19:41

Why? Phil. 2:5-8
He was fully God and fully human (a non-Christian mistake = He was only human. A Christian mistake = He was only God.)

Discuss it . . .
1. What do the passages say about Jesus being human? Physically? Emotionally?
2. How does it make you feel that Jesus went through physical and emotional pain?

3. Why is it important for you to remember that Jesus was fully human?
4. Why did God reduce himself to a human level? See Philippians 2:5-8
5. How would you answer a person who said that, "God doesn't really understand what I am going through"?

Pray it...
Ask God to help you understand the nature of God.

Challenge...
Think about what it means to "seek Jesus' face."

Topic 13 - Jesus is my Teacher

- Called himself teacher & Others called him teacher
- Taught by example – Follow me!
- Taught by telling stories – Parables
- Asked hard questions
- Taught "radical stuff" - Sermon on the Mount (Matt. 5)
  - You are light and salt!
  - Be perfect!
  - How can I be perfect?

Read it . . .
Matthew 5, 6 and 7

Discuss it . . .
1. What does salt do? How are we supposed to be salt for the world?
2. How are supposed to be light for the world? What would that look like at your school?
3. What is the law? What is/was its purpose?
4. For each topic; what was the old law? And how did Jesus change it?
   a. Murder
   b. Adultery/lust
   c. Divorce
   d. Oaths
   e. An eye for an eye (revenge)
   f. Treating an enemy
5. How would your life be different if we all

123

lived by these standards?

6. What can you do to start to live by these standards?

7. Is perfection in this possible? How?

Pray it . . . Ask God to show you your imperfections.

Challenge . . . Pray for Jesus to perfect you.

Topic 14 - Jesus is <u>my Lord</u> -Yahweh (master, controller, boss, leader)

Read it . . .
1. He is Lord of creation –Mark 4:35-41 Jesus Calms the Storm
2. He is Lord of people - John 20:24-29 Jesus Appears to Thomas
   a. We must TRUST God - Proverbs 3:5
   b. We must SUBMIT to God – Proverbs 3:6
   c. We must ABIDE IN Jesus - John 15:5

Discuss it . . .
1. What does the word LORD mean to you?
2. Imagine you're on the boat with Jesus and he commands the storm to stop and it does. What would your reaction be?
3. Who are the people in your life that you trust? What makes them trustworthy?
4. What "trust issues" might you have from being "burned" by others?
5. What does Proverbs 3:5-6 mean? In your own words and in practical terms.
6. So what does it mean to "submit" to Jesus? How is that related to "trust?"
7. How can we "abide or remain" in Jesus?
8. In your own words, how can you make Jesus be LORD in your life?

Pray it . . . Pray for each other's needs.

Challenge . . . Memorize Proverbs 3:5-6
Trust in the LORD with all your heart and lean
not on your own understanding. In all your ways
submit to him, and he will make your paths
straight.

Topic 15 - Jesus is my Friend

- What is a friend?
  - Video clip – "Best Friends" – *Thunderpants*
  - Luke 7:34 (In spite of who we are)

Read it . . .
  - John 15:13-17
    - Lays down life;
    - Knows the Master's business
    - Chosen to change the world
  - James 2:23
    - Faith and action
  - James 4:4
    - Not a friend of the world

Discuss it . . .
  1. Describe a perfect friend. Describe your best friend.
  2. How do you become friends with others?
  3. What do friends do for each other? (Faith, trust, action)
  4. Can you be friends with someone who is older, wiser, stronger than you? How would that work?
  5. Jesus chooses you for friendship; How does that make you feel?
  6. What is Jesus' part of the friend relationship?
  7. What is your part?

8. Why does he ask you not to be friends with the world?
9. How do you benefit from a friendship with Jesus?

Pray it . . . Pray for each other's needs.

Challenge . . . Memorize John 15:15 (NIV)
I no longer call you servants, because a servant does not know his master's business. Instead I have called you friends, for everything that I learned from my Father I have made known to you.

Topic 16 - Jesus is my Savior

Jesus loves us! (even as we sin)

- flim clip –*Carjacking*
    - o "Why did the man risk his life to stop the carjacker?
- film clip – *JESUS - Casting the first stone*
    - o Was the woman guilty?
    - o How did Jesus feel about the woman?
    - o What did he say to her?

He saves us!

- film clip – *JESUS - On the cross*
    - o Why is the religious leader quoting Isaiah 53?
    - o What does it mean when Jesus says; "It is accomplished."?

Read it . . .
Romans 5:6-8, John 3:14b-17, 2 Timothy 1:9-10, Titus 3:3-7

Discuss it . . .

1. In the scripture passages, what does it say about us as sinners?
2. What does Jesus mean by . . . "I came not to condemn . . ."
3. In the scripture passages, what does it say about how Jesus feels about us?
4. In the scripture passages, what does it say about Jesus' purpose here on earth?
5. In words a ten year old could

understand, explain who Jesus is and why and how he saves us.

Pray it . . . Ask to be forgiven, to be held in God's hand and given assurance.

Challenge . . . Memorize John 3:14b-17 (NIV)
" . . . so the Son of Man must be lifted up, that everyone who believes may have eternal life in him."
For God so loved the world that he gave his one and only Son, that whoever believes in him shall not perish but have eternal life. For God did not send his Son into the world to condemn the world, but to save the world through him.

Topic 17 - Jesus is my Shepherd

What are sheep like?
Naturally inclined to follow and flock (need 4 or more)
Can learn to recognize a face and voice
Used for food and clothing (sacrificial lamb)

Read it . . .
Psalm 23, Matthew 9:36, John 10:2-17,
1 Peter 2:25, Revelation 7:17

Discuss it . . .
1. How do sheep act?
2. How might we be like that?
3. How does a shepherd act?
4. What was the shepherd's rod used for?
5. What was the shepherd's staff used for"
6. How does Jesus act as a shepherd to us?

Pray it . . . Pray the 23rd Psalm

Challenge . . . Pick a favorite line from the 23rd Psalm and put it into your own words. (i.e. – Jesus takes care of me by . . .)

The Kingdom of God

Topic 18 - Jesus' Core message = the "Kingdom of God"

Read it . . .
<u>What</u> is the Kingdom of God? (Luke 4:43, John 10:10b)

> Not a location!
>
> It is now! Mark 1:15
>
> It is authority and power! Luke 7:18-22, John 14:12
>
> It grows (parable of the mustard seed)

<u>Where</u> is the Kingdom of God?

> "on <u>earth</u> as it is in <u>heaven</u>" Mt.6:10
>
> John18:36-37 = literally "my <u>authority</u> is not of this world"
>
> God's <u>presence</u> is (in our hearts) = (in our midst) It impacts actions, thoughts, relationships, families, institutions; everything!

Discuss it . . .
1. What was Jesus' life purpose? Luke 4:43 & John 10:10b
2. Define the "Kingdom of God."
3. What kinds of power did Jesus display? Why did he display this power?
4. What does John 14:12 mean to you?
5. Where does this power and authority come from?

Pray it . . . Pray for each other's needs.

Challenge . . . If Jesus is in your heart (your midst), how can others see the Kingdom of God in you?

Topic 19 - When and How is the Kingdom of God coming?

Read it . . .

It is now! Mark 1:15, Matt. 12:28, Luke 17:20-21

It is in the future! Matt. 6:10, Matt. 8:11-12, Is. 25:6, Matt. 26:29

It grows (Mark 4:30-32 parable of the mustard seed)

It is already here in the presence of Jesus and not yet! (pregnancy & parenthood; engagement & marriage)

How is the Kingdom of God coming?

Not by force – Matthew 5:3-10, 39-41, 44 Not in strength but weakness, not in military power but defeat, not in hatred but in sacrificial love. By a Messiah, suffering and crucified – Jesus drank the cup of wrath (God's judgment) on the cross for us. The temple is no longer the source of salvation (torn curtain)

How do we respond?

BE A RADICAL SERVANT EXAMPLE OF FAITH

1. Live each moment in the reality of the Kingdom! – RADICAL
2. Take up our cross and follow Jesus! – SERVANT
3. Live as salt and light! - EXAMPLE
4. Live in present power and future hope of resurrection! - FAITH

Discuss it . . .

1. Using the scriptures page, explain how the Kingdom of God is <u>now</u>.
2. Using the scriptures page, explain how the Kingdom is <u>not yet</u>.
3. Give examples from Matthew 5 of how the Kingdom comes <u>in weakness, defeat, and sacrificial love.</u>
4. Give some everyday examples of how you can . . .

    Be a radical servant example of faith!
   (See Matthew 5)

    a. Radically live in the reality of the Kingdom . . .
    b. Live as a servant following Jesus . . .
    c. Be an example of the Kingdom of God for others . . .
    d. Live in the power and hope of a strong faith . . .

Pray it . . . for the <u>courage</u> to be a radical servant who is an example of faith.

Challenge . . . Live as salt and light.

Topic 20 - How does Jesus "proclaim" the Kingdom of God?

Read it . . .
- Statement of fact – Mark 1:15
- Explanations – Mark 10:14-15, Luke 17:20-21, Matthew 19:13-15
- Parables – Mark 4:30-32, Matthew 20:1-16
- Miracles – (demonstrated its presence; casting out demons, healings, walking on water) Luke 4:40-41, Mark 9:17-27
- His example - (ate with sinners, washed feet, last supper)

Discuss it . . .
1. What is Jesus trying to explain in Mark 10:14-15? Put it in your own words.
2. In the parable of the Workers in the Vineyard (Matt. 20) what is the point of the story?
3. How would you apply that story today?
4. What might have been some reasons for the miracles that Jesus did?
5. In the story of the father and son who needed healing, how was faith involved?
6. How much faith from the father did it take for Jesus to heal the son?
7. What do all these passages teach you about Jesus and the Kingdom of God?

Pray it . . . Ask God to help you proclaim His Kingdom.

Challenge . . . Be an example for others to follow this week.

Topic 21 - The Kingdom of God cares about the LOST.

Read it . . .

Luke 15

> Introduction – What is a parable? Why did Jesus teach with parables?

Read the parable of the Lost Sheep.

Read the parable of the Lost Coin.

Watch the video of the <u>Skit Guys</u> on the *Prodigal Son.*

What do these stories have to do with "welcoming sinners and eating with them"?

Discuss it . . .

1. What is the heavenly message in the parable of . . .
   a. The lost sheep
   b. The Lost coin
   c. The Lost (prodigal) son
2. Who do you normally hang out with? (welcome and eat with)
3. Who today are "lost" people?
   a. In our world?
   b. In our neighborhood?
   c. In your school?
4. Make an argument for welcoming and eating with the lost people you know?
5. How might your parents argue that point? (Would they like you "hanging out" with those kids?)

6. Can you both protect yourself and reach out to the lost? HOW??

Pray . . . Ask God to show you who to reach out to this week.

Challenge . . . Eat with a sinner/outcast this week.

Topic 22 - What is the "real" Kingdom?

Relationship <u>with</u> God.
What are you willing to give up for the Kingdom??

Read it . . .
Parable #1 & 2 – Hidden Treasure & Pearl of Great Price -Matthew 13:44-46
Parable # 3 – The rich fool – Luke 12:16-21
Story – The rich young man – Matthew 19:16-30

Discuss it . . .
1. What is your most valuable possession? Why?
2. Besides physical "stuff," who or what is valuable to you?
3. What or who do you most desire to have in the future?
4. Why were the treasure hunter and the pearl merchant willing to trade everything they had for the ONE thing they most desired?
5. What was foolish about the rich man? (in Luke)
6. Why did the young rich man (Matthew 19) go away sad?
7. How do you think Jesus felt about him?
8. What hope did Jesus give His disciples after the young man walked away?

Pray it . . . Ask God to show you His priorities.

Challenge . . . If you were to really put following God first, what would you be willing to give up?

Topic 23 – Kingdom parables - Attitudes

Read it . . .

- Humility – Parable of the Pharisee and the tax collector - Luke 18:9-14, James 3:13-18, Philippians 2:3-4
- You tube video – Audio Adrenaline – *Get Down*
- Forgiveness – Parable of the Unmerciful Servant – Matthew 18:23-35, Matthew 6:14-15
- Video clip – "Why are you doing this?" - *Fireproof*

Discuss it . . .

1. What are the differences in the way the Pharisee and the taxman prayed?
2. Describe each man's "attitude."
3. How does James suggest we "live humbly?"
4. What does it mean to "humble yourself?"
5. What are the differences in the way the King and the servant treated people who owed them money?
6. How is your forgiveness related to forgiving others?
7. How are humility and forgiveness related?

Pray it . . . Pray for an attitude of humility and forgiveness.

Challenge . . . How can you show humility this week? Who do you need to forgive this week?

Topic 24 - Real Christians vs. Nominal Christians (acting or being something in name only, but not in reality)

Read it . . .
The Parable of the Mustard Seed - Mark 4:30-32
> Birds (nominal Christians) will rest in the branches.

The Parable of the Weeds - Matthew 13:24-43
> Until judgment day; it may be hard to tell the difference between real and nominal Christians.

> "Real" and Nominal Christians - Matthew 7:15-23

Discuss it . . .
1. How do Nominal Christians hide themselves in churches? Why do they do that?
2. Why is it hard to tell a real Christian from a phony one?
3. Can you give an example of someone who is a Christian "in name only?" (no names)
4. Describe what a "real" Christian is like.
5. What does Christian "fruit" look like? (See Galatians 5:22)
6. Why do you come to church?

Pray it . . . Pray for discernment is choosing friends.

Challenge . . . How do you know if you are a "real" Christian or "nominal" Christian?

Topic 25 - Kingdom Parables – Growing fruit

Read it . . .
The seeds that produce a crop - Matthew 13:3-9, 18-23
The barren fig tree – Luke 13:6-9
The vine and the branches – John 15:1-8

Discuss it . . .
1. What does it mean to be fruitful?
2. Put in your own words how Jesus explained the Parable of the Sower.
3. What made the difference in how the different seeds grew?
4. Why did the master want to cut down the fig tree?
5. Why did he let the tree survive for at least another year?
6. Where does a "branch" get its life?
7. What is the difference in a branch that bears fruit and one that doesn't?
8. How do you "abide" in Jesus?
9. What kind of "fruit" does God want you to produce? (Galatians 5:22-23)
10. What can you do to let God produce fruit in you?

Pray it . . . Pray for one of the Spiritual fruits (Galatians 5:22-23) to be displayed in you.

Challenge . . . Memorize the fruits of the Spirit.
(Galatians 5:22-23)

Topic 26 -Talents

Read it . . .
Matthew 25:14-30
What is the point of the parable?
Wing clips DVD
Gifted Hands – TV (don't waste; develop)
Gifted Hands – It's a miracle (We are all miracles)
What do you think happened between the 1st clip and the 2nd?
The Mighty Macs – You have the gift (watch out for distractions)

Discuss it . . .
1. Put the parable of the talents into your own words.
2. Think about the two clips from *Gifted Hands* . . .
3. Did the two boys have any idea what their gifts might be?
4. Did their mother?
5. Why did she insist on limiting their TV watching and making them read books?
6. After seeing the one boy get into John's Hopkins Medical school what do you think the effect that his mother had on him?
7. How do you think the girl felt when her coach said that she had a "gift?"
8. Have you ever been told (like the girl in the clip) that you have a gift? How did that make you feel?

9. Are you a miracle? What are the gifts or talents that God has given you?
10. What are you doing or need to do to discover them?
11. What are you doing to develop them?

Pray it . . . Pray for God to show you your talents.

Challenge . . . Try something new. You may discover a talent.

Resources to Take You Deeper

The Path by Laurie Beth Jones – This is a book that, through some exercises, guides you to write your own personal mission statement. It really helped me to focus on who I was, what I had done in my life so far and come up with what I was all about in terms of ministry.

The Me I Want to Be by John Piper – This is a great book to help understand God's best version of you.

Only You Can be You and *S.H.A.P.E.* - Eric Rees has written two great books to understand your purpose in life. These are based on Rick Warren's thoughts on a purposeful life.

The Way I'm Wired by Katie Brazelton and Joshua Griffen – This is a 6 week video curriculum for a small group. It covers a lot of self discovery issues from spiritual gifts to motives, strengths, weaknesses, and writing your dream statement.

The Way I'm Wired - Katie has also written a devotional, with the same title, that covers these topics throughout the whole Bible.

How Your Teenager is Wired – Katie wrote this version to help parents understand and help their own kids.

A Leaders Life Purpose by Tony Stoltzfus – This is a guidebook/workbook that gives great discovery tools to help one discover their life's calling and purpose.

The Calling Journey - Tony has also written this other book that is really helpful for seeing your life path in the perspective of the lives of many Biblical characters. It will give young people hope in their future and help us older folks understand the peaks and valleys we have endured.

The Landing –This is the curriculum for teens from Saddleback Church's *Celebrate Recovery* program. It is an 8 step Christian version of the 12 step programs that exist for helping people overcome addictions. I have found that this really helps struggling teens to understand God and themselves and their relationships. It is a great yearlong weekly program that is applicable for **all teens**, not just those with addiction issues.

Afterward

This book is primarily written from a Christian worldview. The strategies described here (to embrace, envision and inspire), are based on the Christian Bible.

I do believe, however, that Christian principles will work in the secular world. I see this in sales, education, leadership, parenting and any other endeavor that needs to motivate people.

I was recently (and unhappily) listening to a sales pitch for a timeshare condominium. The salesman spent the first part of the presentation getting to know us. By his "schmoozing" he was embracing us and building a positive relationship. He then moved to getting us to see (envision) what the life style of resort vacationing looked like. He even gave himself as an example of a happy condo owner (an offer of inspiration).

As a football coach, in a public school setting, I found that to motivate my players I needed to embrace them, give them a vision for their role on the team and for what I knew was a winning philosophy in football and in life. Finally, I needed to be an inspirational example of the hard work and enthusiasm that I was teaching them.

As a teacher, I needed to let kids know that I cared personally for them. I tried to help them envision what was needed for success in my classes as well as in their future. I needed to be an inspirational role model and show the enthusiasm and skills that would lead to academic success.

The strategies to embrace, envision and inspire the next generation work in all kinds of situations. It is basic to human interaction and motivation. We cannot limit God's principles to the church only. I invite all, Christian or not, who wish to influence the next generation to consider the strategies in this book.

About the Author

Ben Erickson has spent over forty-three years working with the next generation. He taught high school social studies for twenty years. During that time he coached football and wrestling. He then became a junior high school counselor for ten years. After thirty years in the public schools he became a youth pastor for the next five years. He then returned to the public schools for four years as a special education teacher working with both Asperger's spectrum students and those with behavior disorder issues. He rounded out his career with another four years as a Youth Pastor.

Ben earned his Bachelor's degree from Pacific Lutheran University in 1969 and his Master's in Counseling in 1989 from the University of Puget Sound. In 2012 he became a certified Life Coach through Life Breakthrough Academy.

Ben married his high school sweetheart, Marqua, in 1967. They have two grown daughters, Kristi (Carl) and Tessa and five amazing granddaughters, Amanda, Peyton, Madison, Lauren and Mickela.

Ben's email is ben@lifecoachben.com.

17246219R00094

Made in the USA
San Bernardino, CA
06 December 2014